Men-at-Arms • 510

Dutch Armies of the 80 Years' War 1568–1648(1):

Infantry

Bouko de Groot • Illustrated by Gerry & Sam Embleton
Series editor Martin Windrow

First published in Great Britain in 2017 by Osprey Publishing
PO Box 883, Oxford, OX1 9PL, UK
1385 Broadway, 5th Floor, New York, NY 10018, USA
E-mail: info@ospreypublishing.com

Osprey Publishing, part of Bloomsbury Publishing Plc
© 2017 Osprey Publishing Ltd.

All rights reserved. Apart from any fair dealing for the purpose of private study, research, criticism or review, as permitted under the Copyright, Designs and Patents Act, 1988, no part of this publication may be reproduced, stored in a retrieval system, or transmitted in any form or by any means, electronic, electrical, chemical, mechanical, optical, photocopying, recording or otherwise, without the prior written permission of the copyright owner. Enquiries should be addressed to the Publishers.

A CIP catalogue record for this book is available from the British Library

Print ISBN: 978 1 47281 911 6
PDF ebook ISBN: 978 1 47281 912 3
ePub ebook ISBN: 978 1 47281 913 0

Editor: Martin Windrow
Index by Mark Swift
Typeset in Helvetica Neue and ITC New Baskerville

Originated by PDQ Media, Bungay, UK
Printed in China through Worldprint Ltd

17 18 19 20 21   10 9 8 7 6 5 4 3 2

Osprey Publishing supports the Woodland Trust, the UK's leading woodland conservation charity. Between 2014 and 2018 our donations are being spent on their Centenary Woods project in the UK.

To find out more about our authors and books visit **www.ospreypublishing.com**. Here you will find extracts, author interviews, details of forthcoming events and the option to sign up for our newsletter.

Acknowledgements

The author would like to thank the staff of the Koninklijke Bibliotheek (Royal Library), the Koninklijke Verzamelingen, Archief (Royal House, Archives), and the Nationaal Archief (National Archives), all in The Hague, for their superb assistance.

Picture credits: KB = Koninklijke Bibliotheek, KV = Koninklijke Verzamelingen, and RM = Rijksmuseum, Amsterdam.

Author's Note

On 4 October 1582 the Gregorian calendar that we now use *began* to replace the Julian calendar: when Italy, Portugal, Spain and Poland woke up the next day, it was 15 October. Other countries followed, but at different dates: in the Netherlands the States General, Brabant, Groningen, Holland, Zeeland and the southern provinces did so between December 1582 and February 1583 (although Groningen switched back to the Julian system in November 1594); the other provinces, and the Republic itself, waited until 1700–01. Dates given in this text are those used in current Dutch books.

There is only so much that one can stuff into 48 pages; inevitably, many diagrams, details, banners and interesting anecdotes did not make the cut, but these will find a place on the author's website www.80YW.org.

Artist's Note

Readers may care to note that the original paintings from which the colour plates in this book were prepared are available for private sale. All reproduction copyright whatsoever is retained by the Publishers. All enquiries should be addressed to:
www.gerryembleton.com

The Publishers regret that they can enter into no correspondence upon this matter.

OPPOSITE **Maurice, Prince of Orange, Count of Nassau (1567–1625), portrayed at the age of 30. Because Spain kept William of Orange's eldest son imprisoned in Madrid, the responsibility for continuing their father's work fell to Maurice after William's assassination. Maurice credited as his mentor Justus Lipsius, dean of Leiden University, under whom he studied the classical Roman military literature which formed a basis for the army reforms that he began while still in his twenties. Maurice himself wrote several mathematical treatises in collaboration with Simon Stevin (1548–1620), a leading mathematician, inventor, engineer and author who – as the army's quartermaster – designed its fortifications.**

   Maurice never married, and his first priority was always the security of the nation. His lifelong guiding principles were moderation, balance and discipline, in daily life, politics and military affairs. He was several times offered the sole rule of the new state, but always declined it. In war he abhorred open-field battles: unlike sieges, their outcome was unpredictable, never decisive, yet usually bloody. Nevertheless, his victory at Nieuwpoort (1600) brought him international celebrity: when he was in the field he would be surrounded by dignitaries from many nations seeking to learn from him. (Hondius, 1597; RM)

DUTCH ARMIES OF THE 80 YEARS' WAR 1568–1648 (1):

INFANTRY

INTRODUCTION

On 1 April 1572 several Dutch ships manned by rebels against mighty Spain (which contemptuously called such men 'sea-beggars') chased down an enemy vessel close to shore off Den Briel, a small town not far across the Old River Meuse, south west from Rotterdam. Perhaps because the wind prevented them from returning to the open sea, they decided – several weeks earlier than planned – to start executing their part in a grand scheme to invade the Spanish-occupied Netherlands. Men went ashore and demanded that the town open its gates, 'or else'. As luck had it, most of the town's menfolk were away fishing; the town's council and its Spanish garrison of around 100 men left within hours, afraid that 'or else' would happen anyway. By that evening, around 25 ships had landed 1,400 sea-beggars led by Willem Blois van Treslong, who had been born and raised there, and instead of plundering they quickly set about hauling guns ashore to bolster the town's defences. Around 800 of them then took to their ships again, to look for trouble elsewhere.

Meanwhile, six companies of Spanish veterans under Don Fernando de Toledo were marching hard from Utrecht to Delftshaven (now part of Rotterdam). From there they were shipped across the river to attack Den Briel, but as they marched towards the town a force of sea-beggars suddenly appeared in their rear to burn their vessels. With no way back, Don Fernando had no choice but to order an attack, which failed. Two carpenters from the town then swam to a sluicegate to open it, flooding the land and forcing the attackers onto a narrow dike. Confined without ships on a narrow strip of dry land, the Spanish had no hope of retaking the well-defended town, and they retreated.

The news spread quickly – as did the sea-beggars – and within days nearby towns were occupied by rebels. The day after the Spanish attack on Den Briel other sea-beggars took the port of Veere in Zeeland by surprise; this was the local arsenal for the Spanish navy, and all of its stores and guns fell into rebel hands. By the end of April nearby Antwerp was cut off from the sea, and by mid May towns all over Holland had either been occupied by rebels or had declared for the rebel cause. In France another rebel force had started its part in the grand scheme, taking Mons. But it all started at Den Briel, where the rebels had finally created a foothold on Dutch soil from which they would never be driven.

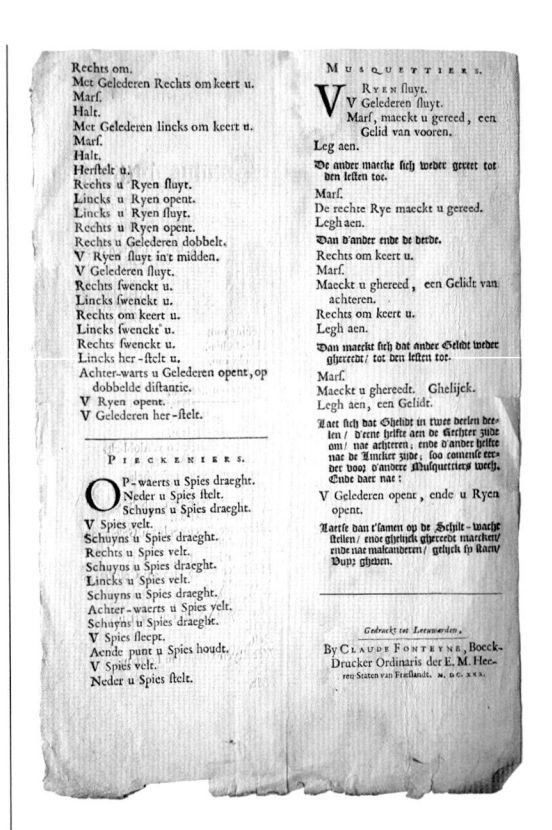

The secret of success: standard commands for controlling a drilled army. Maurice's new methods drew many hundreds of foreign officers to the Netherlands to learn their trade in what Henry Hexham, in his Principles of the Art Military *(1642), called 'this academy and foundation of war', and Maurice's principles became the bedrock of Western military practice for at least 250 years.*

This document is a handy fold-up list of all the commands used in the army of Maurice's half-brother and successor, Frederick Henry of Nassau, from 1630. It is roughly A4 size, printed on both sides, and was widely reproduced; this is the Dutch-language version, but it was also printed in German, French, English and Scottish. To compare the last two, some examples of English vs Scottish commands are: 'Turn to the right hand' vs 'Rictst round about'; 'Files as you were' vs 'Your strings to their first order'; and 'Buck your pikes' vs 'Ondere your pikes'. (KV A23-323)

BACKGROUND

The Habsburg inheritance

When the Holy Roman Emperor and Habsburg monarch Charles V abdicated in 1556 he divided his vast territoties between his younger brother, Ferdinand and his son, Philip; Ferdinand inherited his German possessions as the Emperor, and Philip became King of Spain.[1] Thirty years previously Charles had acquired rule over Artois, Flanders and Burgundy by a short-lived treaty with King Francis I of France; Philip II now inherited these lands as Lord of the Netherlands (but as neither their king, nor their emperor). These were the violent years of the Counter-Reformation; the King of Spain was a devout Catholic, and in the Netherlands he overrode the traditional rights of the local council of nobles (the States General) by unleashing the Inquisition, which condemned to death, by burning at the stake, any who dared to follow the new Protestant faith. The many dukes, counts and wealthy cities that held lands and power in these regions had always enjoyed a semi-independent status, and the initial aim of the revolution that swept the 17 provinces of the Netherlands from 1566 was to secure religious freedom and a certain level of autonomy. At first the rebels did not seek to achieve actual independence, and many still proclaimed their loyalty to the king as their temporal overlord.

On 5 April 1566 a petition was humbly offered to the king's representative in Brussels by hundreds of deliberately unarmed nobles, who appealed for an end to religious persecution and the recognition of the prerogatives of the States General. The tone of this appeal earned them the nickname 'Beggars' – given in disdain, but later accepted with pride. Their request for moderation was at first granted, perhaps because the Netherlands were already in the grip of a rare famine caused by harsh winters and stalled grain imports. However, that same year a rage of Protestant religious iconoclasm swept from city to city, smashing Catholic symbols, as more and more people demanded religious freedom. Valenciennes and Doornik openly declared for Calvinism, and were brutally punished for it. In protest at this, several nobles refused to renew their oath of loyalty to the king's representative. Among them was William, Prince of Orange, Count of Nassau and Buren, the highest ranking aristocrat in the Netherlands. To restore royal authority Madrid sent as the new governor Fernando Alvarez de Toledo, Duke of Alva, with an army of Spanish veterans marched up from Italy.[2] Alva had calculated that he needed to execute 800 noblemen to snuff out opposition and revive the work of the Inquisition.

Many aristocrats fled the Netherlands before his arrival in August 1567, but others, believing that their legal prerogatives and high rank

---

[1] In this text most names are Anglicized for simplicity – in original sources they may appear in contradictory Latin, Flemish, French, Spanish or German forms.
[2] 'Alba' in Spanish sources – the phonetic pronunciation, and the usual form in northern European sources, is 'Alva', so we follow that spelling here.

under the Empire would protect them, chose to stay. These men were summoned, arrested, found guilty, and eventually executed in their many hundreds; those who had fled were also condemned in their absence by Alva's 'Bloody Council', and their lands and possessions, too, were confiscated. These included William of Orange, even though his status under the Empire meant that he could not legally be judged and certainly not punished by the King of Spain, let alone by a mere duke. (It was said at the time that since 'cunning William' had escaped, Alva's joy would be short-lived.) Going one giant step further, on 26 February 1568 the Spanish king declared everyone in the Netherlands, even loyal Catholics, to be heretics: a whole population had been outlawed, leaving them entirely subject to the mercy or otherwise of Madrid's governor-general. William could no longer sit idly by, and he and his brothers recruited two armies to try to liberate the provinces from Alva's tyranny. On 23 May 1568 his brother Louis' army met and soundly defeated a smaller Spanish force at Heiligerlee in the north-east. Traditionally, that was the day the 80 Years' War began.

Terror and defiance

This first rebel invasion failed, and its leaders fled abroad once more. After vengefully restoring order, Alva proposed in 1569 to introduce new taxes to pay for his army: a once-for-all tax of 1 per cent on every possession, a continuing 5 per cent sales tax on land, and a 10 per cent sales tax on everything else. This further alienated peasants, burghers, cities and land-owning nobility alike, but from 1571 the governor demanded payment, using force to collect it if necessary. With so much discontent the time seemed right for the rebels to try again, starting with Den Briel on that fateful 1 April 1572. Alva now tried to cow the rebels by murdering not just individuals, but thousands of townspeople, both Catholic and Protestant, in selected cities in each region (in the south, at Mechelen in October, and in the east, at Zutphen in November). His terror tactics worked, and in December the citizens of Naarden, near

Protestant rebels might wear a 'beggar's medal' to show their hatred of Catholic and Spanish repression. This one dating from 1574 is inscribed 'LIVER TVRCX ** DAN PAVS', or 'Rather Turkish than Papist' – hence the Muslim crescent shape. (RM)

'The Father of the Fatherland': William, Prince of Orange, Count of Nassau-Dillenburg, Count of Buren, Knight of the Golden Fleece (1533–84), portrayed here in his forties. His face is careworn: the burden of leadership of an often squabbling coalition of provinces was relentless, and he lost three of his four brothers in the early battles of the rebellion. Through his first marriage this nobleman of multinational background gained many more rich estates in the Netherlands, and thus their titles and influence. Despite being known to history as 'William the Silent' (due to a later German mistranslation of the Latin *astutus*, 'cunning'), he was in fact anything but taciturn, being witty, quite the romantic, and a skilled diplomat. Apart from his political talents he was also a competent soldier and organizer; a favourite of Emperor Charles V, King Philip II's father, he had been made a lieutenant-general when only 20 years old. One of the most admired figures in early modern European history, William was famously memorialized centuries later in these words: 'As long as he lived he was the guiding star for a whole brave nation, and when he died the little children cried in the streets.' (Wiericks after Goltzius, 1577; RM)

Amsterdam, opened the gates after being promised they would be spared – but Alva's son Don Frederick Alvarez de Toledo broke his word, and had all the townsmen massacred.

After this example other cities in Holland, whatever their religion or politics, refused to let any Spanish in. After a seven-month siege Haarlem fell, and its garrison were slaughtered. Next was Alkmaar in the north, but so many Spanish soldiers had died in the camps around Haarlem that Alva's army soon abandoned this siege and retreated. Then it was the turn of Leiden in the south, which refused to surrender despite one-third of the population dying from hunger. Offered promises of quarter, Leiden kept its gates closed, replying with a quotation from Cato: 'Sweet the fowler's tune when heard – it's merely so to catch the bird.' On land, the rebels had been defeated time and again, but in the coastal waters the odds were reversed. Holding the naval initiative, the 'sea-beggars' exploited their relative strength to relieve Leiden, and after a 12-month siege they succeeded; Spain's hegemony had been successfully challenged.

Then (in the terms of modern chaos theory), 'a butterfly fluttered its wings'. William wanted to reward the city for its courageous resistance with either a new town hall or a university, and Leiden chose the latter. Its new dean was Joost Lips, aka Justus Lipsius (1557–1606), a leading classical scholar and student of Roman military literature; he was also the teacher of William's son Maurice of Nassau, later Prince of Orange. It was Maurice who would combine classical theory and modern practice to create a new army – an army that would defeat the Spanish and their allies, and which became the blueprint for the armies that subsequently allowed the West to conquer the world.

Independence – first unwanted, then proclaimed

Not long after Leiden, the initial anti-Spanish unity among the provinces broke down due to mutual suspicions, and a polarization of religious differences between the Protestant and Catholic camps (themselves each divided internally between fundamentalists and moderates). Despite William's proposals for unity based on religious toleration, the Catholic provinces in the south (roughly, parts of modern northern France and the southern Netherlands, Belgium and Luxembourg) created an anti-Calvinist alliance in 1579, and then signed a peace with Spain. In the north (roughly, the modern Netherlands), several provinces also created their own Protestant alliance. A year later William was branded an outlaw by Spain.

Realizing that Philip II would never agree to religious freedom, on 26 July 1581 the northern alliance published their declaration of independence. This stated, in part, that if a ruler, placed by God at the head of his subjects, oppressed them and took away their established privileges and liberties, and if his subjects had been unable to appease him by 'submissive demonstrations', ' then he must be treated as a tyrant and abandoned… Let it be known that we… have declared, to the King of Spain… that his rule, justice and inheritance of these lands are annulled.'

However, in a world where nationhood was still synonymous with monarchy, the northern alliance then looked for a new king who would respect their rights. Between 1581 and 1586 royal figures in England, France and Austria were all invited to accept this role, but these

An officer and a gentleman, 1620s; note his hat brim extravagantly turned up, long feather plumes, and broad lace collar. Nobility was not a prerequisite for becoming an officer in the States' Army, but it helped. High birth brought a better network of contacts and more access to funds, which ensured a steadier flow of replacement recruits, and a cushion when government pay was late. However, during the course of the 80 Years' War the percentage of noblemen among captains and lieutenants declined steadily, and by the 18th century this would become very evident when compared to the armies of other nations. (Meyer; RM)

negotiations all failed. In 1584, after many earlier attempts financed by Madrid, William of Orange was assassinated in The Hague. When the last foreign would-be ruler withdrew from discussions in 1587, the rebellious provinces decided to establish the Republic of the Seven United Netherlands (aka the United Provinces). This republic – a radical political innovation at the time – would be governed by the States General, a general assembly of representatives; protected by the *Staatse Leger* (States' Army); and led by at first two and later a single *Stadhouder* ('Stead-Holder' – meaning roughly 'lord steward'), who was also the army's captain-general. The first to fill this national leadership role was William's son Maurice of Nassau, who would be succeeded on his death in 1625 by his half-brother Frederick Henry.

Internationally, the new state would be recognized *de facto* on 31 October 1596, when England and France signed a Triple Alliance with the United Provinces. Spain would not finally recognize it until the Treaty of Münster in 1648, an element of the Peace of Westphalia which ended the pan-European 30 Years' War, with which the 80 Years' War had become partially merged since 1621. By 1648 the Republic created and defended by the one-time rebellious 'beggars' – by their endurance and growing prowess; by charting a skilful course during generations of wars between Spain, France, England and various German states; and by simultaneously funding and pursuing supremacy at sea – had emerged as a global power.

One of the many well-known plates by Jacob de Gheyn, whose book showed the individual arms drill for pike, caliver and musket. Less well known is the name of the world's first 'catalogue model', shown here: Pieter van der Molen (aka Pierre du Moulin), a member of Maurice's bodyguard who was asked to pose for De Gheyn's many plates. As a captain, Van der Molen became master-at-arms of the guard, and in 1622 he was made sergeant-major in the army. Maurice did not at first allow De Gheyn's plates, commissioned in 1596–98 by his cousin John, to be published, because he considered his new methods of drill – for everyone from individual soldiers up to whole armies – to be a 'secret weapon'. It was not until 1608, with peace negotiations for the long truce almost concluded, that permission was granted to publish them. (RM)

Some of Alva's much hated Spanish-Italian soldiers, here a drummer, fifer, sergeant and ensign. They mutinied as often as German mercenaries over lack of pay, but at least they waited until after the battle; many German mutinies broke out shortly before or even during an engagement, usually sealing their and their army's fate. In 1594 a group of 400 Italian mutineers decided to play the long game, and actually set up their own soldiers' republic near Tilburg; it was ruled as a kind of democracy, and internal order was strictly maintained, though they lived by blackmailing and plundering the surrounding countryside under Spanish protection. Because of this, Maurice even signed a defence treaty with them, while Spain tried but failed to defeat them. By the time Spain finally paid and pardoned them two years later their strength had grown to 2,800, speaking 13 languages. Others tried to copy their success four times in the years that followed, even contributing troops to Maurice's siege of 's Hertogenbosch. (De Bruyn, 1581; RM)

The Netherlands during the Eighty Years' War

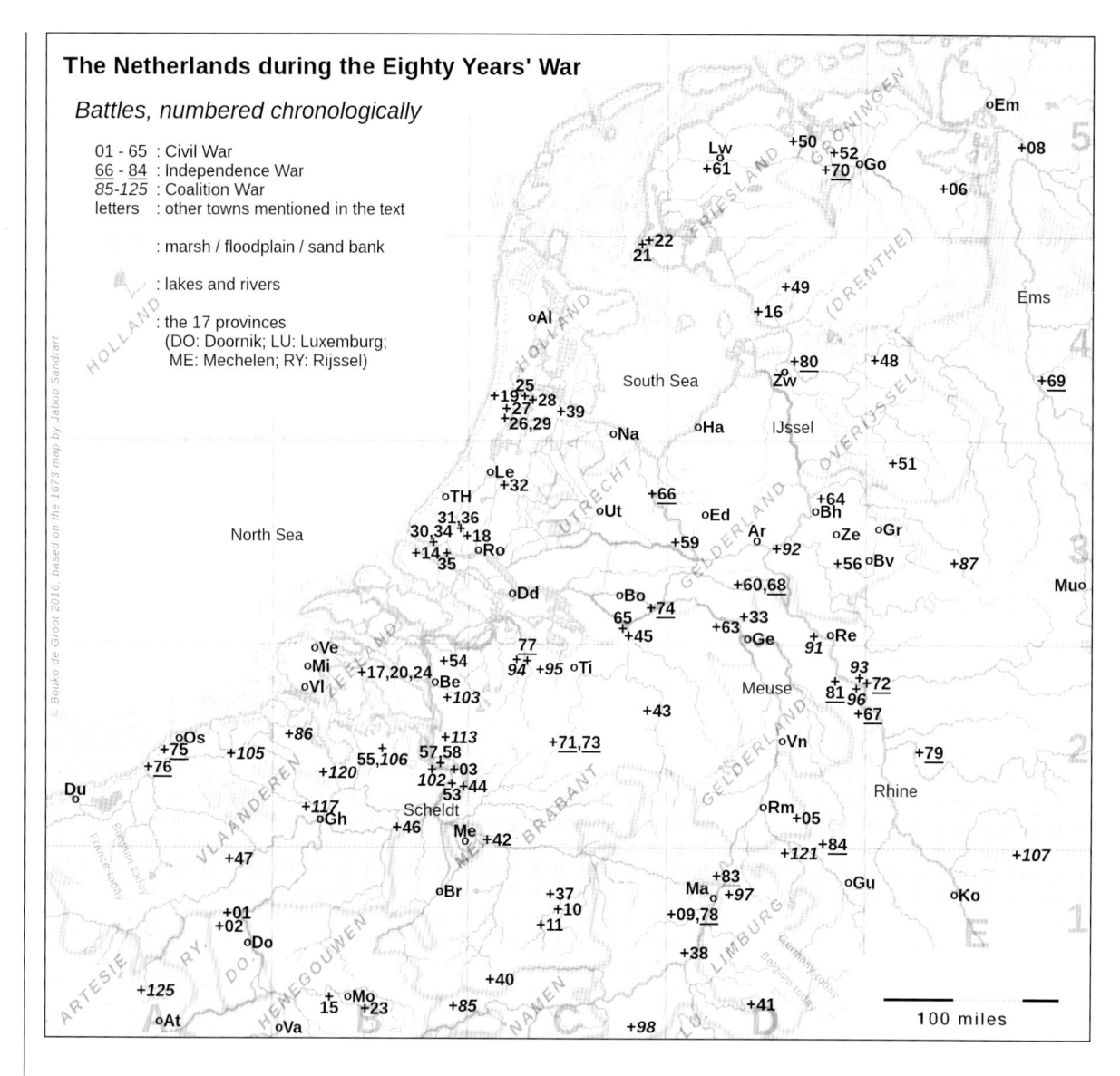

Battles, numbered chronologically

- 01 - 65 : Civil War
- 66 - 84 : Independence War
- 85 - 125 : Coalition War
- letters : other towns mentioned in the text

: marsh / floodplain / sand bank

: lakes and rivers

: the 17 provinces
(DO: Doornik; LU: Luxemburg; ME: Mechelen; RY: Rijssel)

100 miles

On the map, locations of open-field land battles are marked thus – +01, 66, +85, etc. – the numbers corresponding with those in the Chronology text, and the type style indicating period as per the map key. Other cities and towns also mentioned in the text, but not numbered as battles, are identified with a small circle and the following abbreviations; note grid references:

Al = Alkmaar (C4), Ar = Arnhem (D3), At = Atrecht/Arras (A1), Be = Bergen op Zoom (B2), Bo = Bommel (C3), Bv = Bredevoort (E3), Bh = Bronkhorst, (D3) Br = Brussels (B1), Do = Doornik (A1), Dd = Dordrecht (C3), Du = Duinkerken/Dunkirk (A2), Ed = Ede (D3), Em = Emden (E5), Ge = Gennep (D3), Gh = Ghent (B2), Gr = Groenlo (E3), Go = Groningen (D5), Gu = Gulik (D1), Ha = Hardewijk (D4), Ko = Köln/Cologne (E1), Lw = Leeuwarden (D5), Le = Leiden C3), Ma = Maastricht (D1), Me = Mechelen (B2), Mi = Middelburg (B2), Mo = Mons/Berg (B1), Mu = Münster (E3), Na = Naarden (C4), Os = Ostend (A2), Re = Rees (D3), Rm = Roermond (D2), Ro = Rotterdam (C3), TH = The Hague/Den Haag (B3), Ti = Tilburg (C2), Ut = Utrecht (C3), Va = Valenciennes (B1), Ve = Veere (B2), Vn = Venlo (D2), Vl = Vlissingen/Flushing (B2), Ze = Zelhem (D3), Zw = Zwolle (D4). (Author's map)

CHRONOLOGY

The following gives a bare listing of the main events and the open-field battles of the 80 Years' War, the latter numbered as on the accompanying map, with grid squares.

Soon after the start of the war it was realized that it could never be decided by pitched battles; economic control was more important, and that meant control over cities. The aim of most campaigns by both sides was thus to capture, besiege or relieve strategic cities and towns, rather than to meet and destroy enemy armies in the open field. This important positional warfare – sieges, assaults, sallies and captures, decided by artillery, engineering and bloody trench warfare – will be covered in the **forthcoming second volume**, along with the cavalry.

Only actual engagements are listed here; there were numerous episodes of manoeuvre and counter-manoeuvre that did not end in bloodshed, like the many face-offs during the 'Gulik Wars' in Germany – the War of the Jülich Sucession (1609–14), when the United Provinces and Spain supported different sides, but avoided combat due to the 12 Years' Truce between them. (And in 1624 a 3,000-man Spanish raid from Ede to Arnhem is said to have turned back simply because one lone citizen was heard playing the Dutch national anthem on his trumpet.) During the overlapping 30 Years' War phase (1621–48) Catholic armies repeatedly marched up and down the borders shadowed by Protestant forces, with neither initiating engagements. Note, too, that although they are not listed in the Chronology, throughout the war Dutch land campaigns were supported by naval actions – attacks on Spanish ships, landings, relief convoys, raids on ports and Spanish communications, etc. – which were increasingly successful and significant.

While the war's starting date is traditionally accepted as 23 May 1568, the day of the victory at Heiligerlee, 1566 had already seen the Petition of the Beggars, a tide of religious iconoclasm, William of Orange and other senior nobles meeting to discuss armed resistance, and clashes at Waterloo (now Wattrelos, 01 on map) and Lannoy (02, both in grid A1). In 1567 Alva's 'Bloody Council' began its sessions, with 1,000 people executed and 11,000 banished. Many more Protestants fled, to become 'sea-beggars' and 'forest-beggars', and there were encounters at Oosterweel (03, in B2) and Saint-Denis (04).

Civil War, 1568–87

1568 Whole population of the Netherlands declared heretic. First multi-pronged rebel invasion. In the north, actions at 05 Dalheim (D2), 06 Heiligerlee (E5), raid on Brussels, 07 Saint-Valery, 08 Jemmingen (E5), 09 Tongeren (D1), 10 Tienen (Tirlemont, C1), 11 Geldenaken (Jordoigne, C1). William and his brothers retreat into Germany; leading Catholic nobles Counts of Egmont and Horne executed in Brussels.

1569 12 Jarnac, 13 Moncontour (in aid of French Huguenots). Alva announces new taxes.
1570 Second rebel invasion falters before it really starts.
1571 Third invasion likewise aborted; Den Briel targeted.
1572 Fourth rebel invasion succeeds: 14 Den Briel (B3), 15 Saint-Ghislain (B1), 16 Blokzijl (D4), 17 Goes (B2), 18 Overschie (B2), 19 Santpoort (C4), 20 Goes (B2), 21 Stavoren & 22 Koudum (C4), 23 Harmignies (B1), 24 Goes (B2). Spanish massacres in cities, e.g. Mechelen, Zutphen, Naarden.
1572–73 Alva slowly regains control in south and east, besieging Haarlem and cutting Holland in two: 25 Sparendam, 26 Heemstede/ 'Manpad', 27 Haarlem, 28 Diemerdijk, 29 Heemstede/ 'Manpad' (all C4), 30 Maaslandsluis & 31 Poldervaart (B3). Alva replaced by Don Luis de Requesens.
1574 Leiden besieged; 32 Alphen aan de Rijn (C3), 33 Mookerheide (D3), 34 Maaslandsluis, 35 Vlaardingen, 36 Poldervaart (all B3). 'First Spanish Armada', against Holland, falters before it leaves port. 'Bloody Council' stands down.
1575 First peace negotiations fail on religious grounds. Revolt spreads southwards again; more Spanish massacres.
1576 'The Spanish fury': sack of Antwerp by unpaid Spanish soldiers kills c. 8,000 citizens. In response, Protestants and Catholics unite in the **Pacification of Ghent, forming first national army** with mutual religious toleration. 37 Vissenaken (C1).
1577 Complex three-cornered negotiations between States General, William and Spanish governor Don Juan of Austria fail. States General ask Philip II's nephew Archduke Matthias of Austria to rule. 38 Luik/ Liege (D1), 39 Amsterdam (C4).
1578 Religious polarization destroys rebels' unity; government moves from Brussels to Antwerp. 40 Gembloers/ Gembloux (C1), 41 Limburg (D1), 42 Rijmenam (C2). Spanish reconquer south; on Don Juan's death Alexander Farnese (named Duke of Parma from 1586) is appointed governor, serving until 1592.
1579 Parma manipulates religious divisions; **Netherlands divide** between southern, mostly Catholic, royalist Union of Atrecht (Arras), and northern, mostly Protestant, rebellious Union of Utrecht. 43 Woensel (C2), 44 Borgerhout (B2), 45 's Hertogenbosch (C3), 46 Baasrode (B2).
1580 William of Orange outlawed; makes treaty with Duke of Anjou, brother of King of France. 47 Ingelmunster (A1), 48 Hardenberg (E4), 49 Steenwijk (D4)
1581 Matthias of Austria leaves. **Northern provinces declare their independence.** 50 Kollum (D5), 51 Goor (E3), 52 Noordhorn (D5).
1582 Duke of Anjou, offered throne with limited powers, arrives with small French army.
1583 'The French fury'; Anjou's attempted coup in Antwerp fails, and he leaves Netherlands. Government

moves to The Hague. 53 Antwerp, 54 Steenbergen, 55 Hulst (all B2).
1584 William of Orange assassinated. 56 Terborg (D3, part of 'Cologne War').
1585 England sends 6,000 men under Earl of Leicester in official support. **Maurice becomes stead-holder.** Siege of Antwerp – 57 Kouwensteinsedijk & 58 Lillo (B2); 59 Amerongen & 60 Nijmegen (D3).
1586 States General grant Leicester wide powers, but his greed for more, his coup and his military failures destroy his credibility. 61 Boksum (D5), 62 Werl (part of 'Cologne War'), 63 Grave & 64 Warnsveld (D3).
1587 Leicester leaves Netherlands. 65 Engelen (C3).

War for Independence, 1588–1620
1588 The Justification or Deduction is published (government should be exercised by the States General, not by an individual, i.e. the **birth of the Republic**). Anglo-Dutch defeat of 'Second Spanish Armada' sent to transport Parma's army to England.
1589 Spanish defeat of 'English Armada' to Corunna and Lisbon led by Sir Francis Drake. 66 Amersfoort (C3), 67 Rijnberk/ Rheinberg (D2). Spain distracted by French Wars of Religion; Parma leaves for France.
1590 Maurice begins counter-offensive, capturing Breda (C2).
1591 68 Knodsenburg (D3), 69 Lingen (E4).
1593 70 Tolbert D5), 71 Turnhout (C2), Luxembourg expedition.
1595 72 Lippe; first major army exercises; Metz expedition to aid French allies.
1596 Republic recognized by England and France in Triple Alliance. Anglo-Dutch raid on Cadiz.
1597 73 Turnhout (C2).
1598 Death of Philip II, succeeded by Philip III.
1599 74 Heerewaarden (C3).
1600 75 Leffinge (A2), 76 Nieuwpoort (A2) – landmark Dutch victory.
1601 77 Breda (C2).
1602 Foundation of Dutch East Indies Company (VOC). 78 Tongeren (D1).
1605 79 Mühlheim (on the Ruhr, E2).
1606 80 Berkum (D4).
1608 81 Xanten (D2).
1609 Commencement of 12 Years' Truce. 82 Neira (Indonesia).
1610 82 Mechelen (on the Meuse, D1), 83 Erkelenz (D2).
1615 Expedition to Brunswick brings local conflict there to an end.
1618 Outbreak of European 30 Years' War in Bohemia. Religious divisions within Protestant camp endanger unity of Netherlands and its army; separatist tensions in province of Holland.
1619 Execution of Holland's 'prime minister' Van Oldenbarneveldt ends turmoil.
1620 Expedition to Frankfurt to head Protestant armies in 30 Years' War comes to nothing.

Coalition War, 1621–48
1621 End of 12 Years' Truce. Foundation of Dutch West Indies Company (WIC).
1622 85 Fleurus (B1), 86 Oostburg (B2).
1623 87 Stadtlohn (30 Years' War, E3)).
1624 Skirmishers ('*vuurroers*') become official part of the army. 88 Pescadores (Taiwan), 89 San Salvador de Bahia (Brazil).
1625 Death of Maurice, succeeded by Frederick Henry. 90 Elmina (Ghana).
1626 91 Honnepel/ 'Kalkarse Gat' (D3).
1627 Frederick Henry has by now retaken all Netherlands territory north of the major rivers.
1628 Spanish treasure fleet captured off Cuba.
1629 Siege of 's Hertogenbosch, funded by proceeds of the treasure fleet. Spain assisted by Catholic League henceforward. 92 Westervoort (D3), 93 Wesel (D2), 94 Prinsenbeek & 95 Bavel (C2). Government temporarily moves to Utrecht to boost morale.
1630 96 Bunick/ Boenning (D2).
1631 'Third Spanish Armada', against Holland, defeated.
1632 Siege of Maastricht; 97 Ammi (D1).
1634 Offensive/defensive alliance with France; expedition to Luxembourg.
1635 98 Les Avins/ Huy (French in alliance, C1); 99 Taccariang (Taiwan). Frederick Henry commands combined Dutch-French army; government temporarily moves to Arnhem to boost morale.
1636 100 Porto Calvo (Brazil).
1637 101 Porto Calvo.
1638 102 Kallo & 103 Wouw (B2).
1639 'Fourth Spanish Armada', against Holland, defeated; 104 Thionville (French in alliance).
1640 105 Brugge (A2), 106 Hulst (B2), 107 Wipperfurt (E1).
1642 109 Inchy (Dutch-French). 110 Namboa Angongo, Dembos expedition (Angola).
1643 111 Bengo (Angola), 112 Rocroi (French in alliance), 113 Hoogerheide (B2).
1644 114 New Amsterdam/ New York
1645 115 Indecuta (Angola), 116 Tabocas (Brazil) , 117 Landegem (B2).
1646 118 Kavala &119 Muxima (Angola), 120 Molensteeg/ Eeklo (B2; example of international cooperation. While Frederick Henry with a Dutch-French army outmanoeuvres Piccolomini around Antwerp, William's grandson Turenne marches a French-Swedish army along the Rhine).
1647 Death of Frederick Henry, succeeded by William II. 121 Heinsberg (D1), 122 Kombi (Angola).
1648 War formally ends with Peace of Münster. 123 Guararapes (Brazil, and again in 1649), 124 Mbaca (Angola), 125 Lens (A1, French in alliance).

CIVIL WAR, 1568–87

This period was more or less chaotic; it saw many small engagements throughout the country, some of which proved to be more decisive than bigger battles later on. As in all civil wars, particularly those with a religious dimension, engagements of any size tended to be vicious, and Spain's brutal persecution in rebel areas made it even worse. The major limiting factor to military success was money. Mercenary units were needed, because there were not enough local and allied Huguenot (French Protestant) units to create armies large enough to take on the Spanish.

William of Orange had to cope with all the problems from which such armies inevitably suffer: disobedience, drunkenness, plundering, mutiny, desertion, factional fighting, and even attempts on his life. He took great pains to try to pay the troops on time, not to overstretch the country's resources, and to suppress corruption, as did his sons subsequently. William took the first steps towards creating a national army, setting in motion a plan for registration and conscription; he raised the wages of his men, and recruitment commissioners ensured that sergeants were of sufficient quality. Some companies were recruited at 150 per cent of the required strength, so that they could quickly make up any losses. In 1580 it was decided that captains should put their men in battle order once a week to practise manoeuvres. In short, William set the army on a new path, creating the foundations on which Maurice could build his reforms. (After William's death the Earl of Leicester was less concerned with sound finances. As a result his expeditionary army was too large for the funds available, and riddled with corruption; it soon fell apart, even selling towns to the Spanish.)

Organization

The smallest administrative and tactical unit was the company or 'ensign'. (This English term, confusingly, is also used by extension for both a company flag, and the officer who carried it; in Dutch they were *vaandel* and *vaandrig*, respectively). At the start of the conflict these were supposed to be 400 strong, of whom 200 were armed with calivers, 150 with pikes, and 50 with halberds or two-handed swords. In many German units only around one-third of the men had calivers. Walloon companies only mustered about 200 men; Huguenot companies were smaller still, at around 150, and often relied solely on calivers. Having fought with the Huguenots, William of Orange too preferred the use of firearms, and small companies; in 1570 he wrote to his brother John that he would rather have 50 French or Walloon calivermen than 100 *Landsknechts*. Nevertheless, he reduced the 100 per cent firearms ratio to some 70 per cent in 1578, and to 60 per cent a year later. In 1574 he promoted the introduction of the heavier musket by handing them out as gifts to captains. At around the same date he finally completed another, much lengthier process of reform that predated him: the last local companies

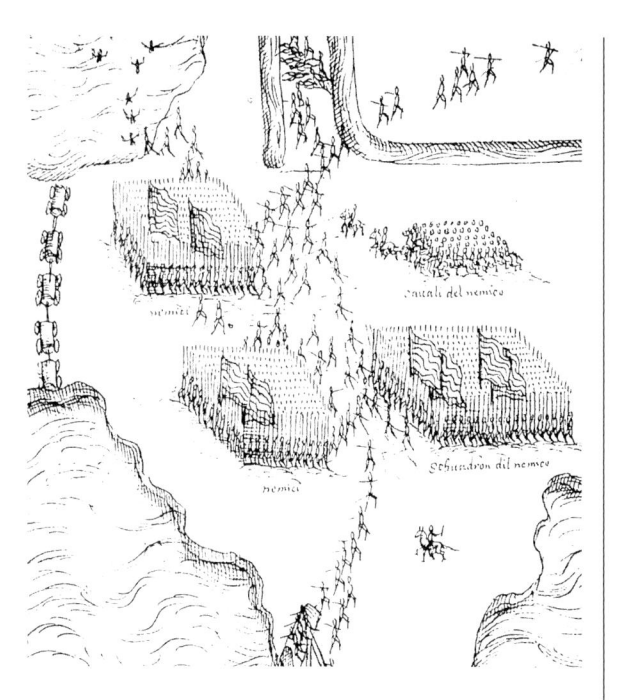

Detail from an event map of the battle of Koudum (10 September 1572), one of a series made for Caspar de Robles, then Stead-Holder of Friesland and Groningen. Rebels attacked Robles' troops as they returned from fighting at Stavoren two days earlier. According to Robles, he had 600 Walloon and 400 German foot (left), the rebels 1,600 foot and 60 horse, many from surrounding cities. The drawing is mostly interesting in showing typically encumbered terrain, with a barricade of wagons (left) and a raised bank (bottom) as well as water obstacles. It supposedly shows the rebel troops partly deployed behind defensive works moments before Robles' troops assaulted and defeated them. (Tresoar, *Histoarysk en Letterkundich Sintrum foar Fryslân te Leeuwarden;* Robles Atlassen nr. 56)

had changed from the old *Landsknecht* organization – with its variable numbers, elected leaders and questionable loyalties – to the new system, with its fixed numbers and ratios and centrally appointed officers.

Thus, from the mid 1570s most companies were either 150 or 200 strong, including a captain, a lieutenant, an ensign, two sergeants, three corporals, two drummers, a fifer and (staying behind in camp) a quartermaster and a barber-surgeon; all of these were classed as 'officers'. The fifer was omitted in smaller companies, and sometimes a provost (in charge of discipline) was added. According to 1580 regulations, the remainder of the 150 men were to consist of 65 calivermen, 12 musketeers, 45 pikemen, six halberdiers, six 'targeteers' (sword-and-buckler men), and three boys as servants for the three senior officers. Several cadets would also serve in the ranks; these were volunteers waiting to be (re-)posted as officers elsewhere, who fought either with sword-and-buckler or pike. The mix of halberdiers and swordsmen might differ, including some men with double-handed swords. Sergeants and corporals were assisted by a number of lance-corporals, the only non-officer rank above common soldier. Whatever their size, companies would carry weapons in similar ratios and have the 13 officers listed above. In times of peace companies would be reduced, e.g. from 150 men to 113 of all ranks. In the midst of a campaign companies below half their 'paper' strength were not uncommon.

Not everyone followed these regulations. Newly mustered foreign companies might still be 300–400 strong, especially the German ones. Such units would be disbanded after a campaign, not reduced. Under Leicester in 1587 English companies of 150 men had more musketeers and halberdiers (and his army also included archers). Frisian companies that year also showed variety: some had 20 per cent halberdiers and two-handed swordsmen plus 50 per cent pikes, but others had 70 per cent firearms. Nevertheless, the trend was clear.

Companies were raised individually and eventually grouped into regiments, mainly for administrative purposes; such a group might not even be called a regiment but merely identified as a 'colonelcy'. The number of companies in a colonelcy or regiment was not fixed. Provincial regiments like the Zeeland Regiment are mentioned right from the start, but still only to indicate the companies then in the pay of that province. In April 1572 the very first complete regiment was raised, by Zeeland; it was English, led by Walter Raleigh's half-brother Humphrey Gilbert. A month later the province of Holland contracted a German, Lazarus Muller, to recruit a regiment from around Bremen and Hamburg. Holland's first Scottish regiment arrived in 1573, led by Andrew Ormiston. All three of these had ten companies.

As the scope and scale of the war escalated, the first local colonels were appointed in 1574, the better to command the many companies in the south of Holland. The first complete regiments mustered locally appear at the same time as the formation of the first national army. In September 1576 the States General formed an army of around 15,000 foot and 10,000 horse, including seven new regiments. The commanding general was Philippe de Croy, Duke of Aerschot, with a staff including a lieutenant-general, a sergeant-major-general, eight councillors of war, and a general of cavalry. This army also included (briefly) the last traces of the old Burgundian organization: 15 '*bandes d'ordonnance*'.

Halberdier bodyguard of Maurice of Nassau, depicted outside the court in The Hague (today's Houses of Parliament). Maurice's father William of Orange and his half-brother Frederick Henry both had the same bodyguard, always dressed like this in sleeved blue cloaks; it may thus be considered as the new nation's first real uniform. Ceremonial touches are the very ornate halberd-heads with added tassels. (Detail from Breen, 1618; RM)

Rebel field armies could be as big as 25,000–30,000, plus about the same number of troops in garrisons. For example, William's field army at the battle of Geldenaken in 1568 had 26,000–28,000 men, including 10,000 Germans and 8,000 French and Walloon foot.

In the field
For major field operations companies were divided according to their weapons, to be regrouped with similarly armed men of other companies. These were then formed into tactical battalions, with firearms flanking a pike block, and ensigns, halberdiers, etc. in its centre. Ideally a single administrative regiment would operate as a single tactical battalion, but in reality companies from different regiments (sometimes even of different nationalities, which reduced the risk of mutiny) were tactically grouped to achieve a practical battalion size of 1,500–3,000 men. It seems that the smallest building-block here was the 'half-corporalship' of 10–15 men under a (lance-)corporal, but men might still be stripped away from these to fill a gap somewhere else. The planning for all this was done in advance, based on experience and manuals. The actual separation and regrouping was done while forming marching columns, each of the required battalion width (on the march) and depth (in the battle line), so that these could then march onto the field of battle in the proper order, to turn and file into their assigned positions. That would take quite some time, and a lot of pushing, shoving and cursing, especially with inexperienced men in a multinational battalion.

Moving a deployed battalion around was an even bigger headache, because it could easily become disordered; halting every 15 paces or so to re-dress the ranks was the only way to solve this. The many ditches, dikes and marshy areas on most of the early battlefields made things even worse: battles were lost because units became disordered (e.g. at Heiligerlee).

Each man in the central pike block would occupy a space of 2–3ft wide (60–90cm) and 3ft deep; on the march this depth would increase to around 7ft (210cm). Calivermen and musketeers needed that double width, to avoid each other's burning matches. Pikemen would usually be deployed either to fill a *square of ground* (e.g. 60ft x 60ft, 18m x 18m, or 30 men wide by 20 men deep); or to form a *square of men* (e.g. 30 x 30 men, or 60ft wide x 90ft deep, 18m x 27m). Commanders might create an extra wide or extra deep formation as circumstances demanded. The many ditches in the terrain forced adjustments, so *squares of men* were used more frequently.

Firearms-men were usually deployed on the pike block's flanks, and often in the same numbers of ranks. They were only lethal up to a range of 80 yards or so, so preferably part of them would spread out in front of the block to skirmish with opponents, using cover where possible. Several men would walk forward, shoot, then walk back to reload, while others then walked forward in their turn, but initially without clear commands or structure. Nevertheless, volleys could be fired, and seem to have become more common during the 1580s, though they were avoided by commanders of green troops. This was to avoid panic during the sudden silence after a volley, and to prevent the rear ranks firing happily into thin air or into the men in front of them. Even when skirmishing, experience was a clear advantage, judging from the low losses Spanish

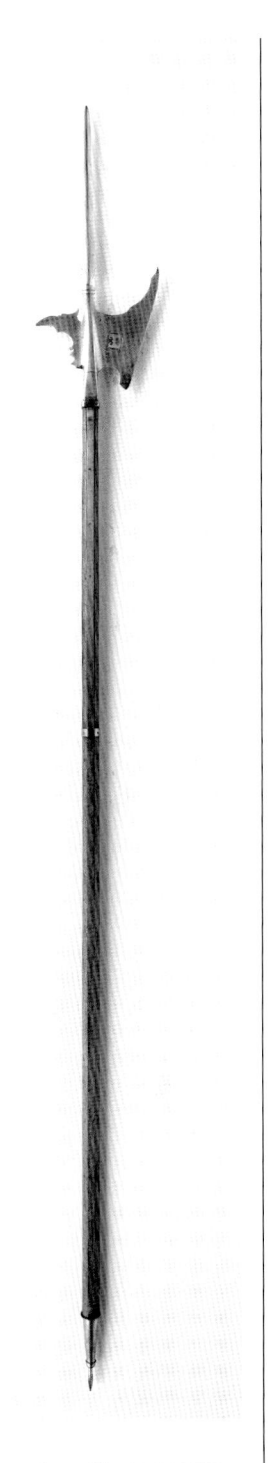

A more workmanlike sergeant's halberd dating from the 17th century, almost 7½ft (230cm) long. Note the spiked ferrule, and the long langets protecting each side of the upper part of the shaft. In 1580 each Dutch mixed-arms company was to have six halberdiers. (RM)

Engraving depicting an inspection of the rebels' army on 14 July 1578 near Antwerp. Six months previously the country's first national army had been routed at Gembloers, but the major Flemish cities were still supporting the rebel cause, and this new army was funded by Holland, Zeeland, Antwerp and Ghent. This situation would soon change, quickly followed by the third exodus of money and brains to Holland, mostly to Amsterdam.

Pike and shot are clearly differentiated in the formations in this meticulously researched plate, and the numbers of companies (*Fenlin*) listed by each match the numbers of flags depicted. The cavalry (second, third and fourth columns from the top) are all identified as '*Schwartze Reuter*' or 'black riders'; the large infantry formations (first and fifth columns) as '*Scotten*'; the leading units in the second and fourth columns as '*Hollanders*'; the left-hand unit in the central column as '*Deutsche knecht*', and the central unit ahead of it as '*Engelsche*'. (Hogenberg, 1580; RM)

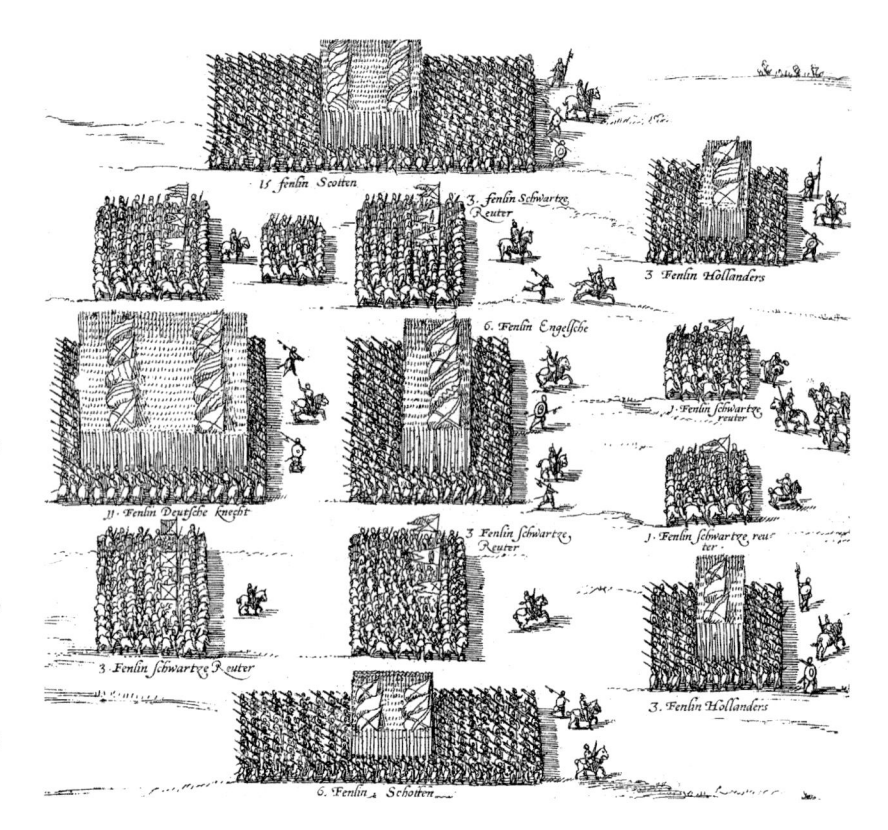

Each company had two drummers; this depiction dates from 1635, but the size of the drums did not really change during the whole period. For their positions in the battle line, see diagram of 500-man division on page 17. (Callot; RM)

troops often suffered during prolonged fire-fights (e.g. at Alphen aan de Rijn and Mookerheide).

Unsurprisingly, faced with these difficulties most commanders preferred a defensive approach, which also took advantage of the excellent cover and protection against cavalry offered by all those ditches and dikes, to say nothing of the opportunities for ambush (e.g. at Noordhorn and Rijmenam). Especially during the hectic first decade, many battles involved only a handful of companies on either side, applying the same basic principles on a smaller scale. There were no fixed organizations for armies, each one being a different amalgamation of the available units.

The soldiers' equipment

At first every man had to provide his own kit, but once things got better organized it was the captain's job to ensure his men were suitably equipped. Often newly mustered troops would receive their first month's pay in cloth or ready-made clothes. Companies would thus look 'uniform', but regiments not mustered as a single entity perhaps less so. If a colour for such issue cloth is mentioned at all, it is usually blue, though green is occasionally mentioned. To distinguish friend from foe plumes could be worn, and (by officers only) sashes. Plumes were usually orange-and-white, orange-white-and-blue, or orange-white-and-green, whereas their royalist opponents often wore red plumes. Sashes showed less uniformity: orange, blue, green, or tricolour orange-white-blue. Even red was used for a while, because – counter-intuitively – during the early period rebels against the Spanish governers still wanted to show their basic loyalty to the Spanish king.

Every man carried a sword and perhaps a dagger. Calivermen carried the lightest equipment: a matchlock caliver, around 4ft (120cm) long, firing bullets of around 20 to the pound weight. The musketeer started to appear in the rebel armies from 1575, carrying a heavier and harder-hitting weapon shooting bullets weighing 12 to the pound. His roughly 5ft-long matchlock musket (150–160cm) weighed around 17lb (8kg), explaining the need for him to carry a forked rest. He carried a dozen or so pre-measured charges in small wooden or metal cylinders suspended from a shoulder belt (hence 'the 12 apostles'). Although a musket hit harder than a caliver, it used about twice as much powder, and had roughly half the rate of firing. The caliverman carried a flask of powder, and both types of soldier a separate flask of finer priming powder, a bag of lead bullets, a cleaning set and plenty of matchcord (which burned at a rate of about 10ins/ 25cm per hour). Firearms-men might wear a helmet, although regulations did not require them.

Pikemen were expected to have a helmet (of one of many types), a full iron back-and-breast corselet, and a pike 15–18ft (5–6m) long. But corselets were heavy and long pikes unwieldy, so to lighten his 33lb (15kg) load by half many a pikeman left his detachable arm and thigh plates at home, and considerably shortened his weapon. Halberdiers and swordsmen were also required to be armoured. Officers might even purchase a shotproof corselet, at ten times the price of a normal one. Officers would carry a partisan, sergeants – and for a while, corporals – a halberd.

Although they are not mentioned in any regulation, an experienced company probably had several sharpshooters, perhaps equipped with rifled hunting calivers or even the occasional wheellock rifle. Another way to hit harder was to cut the lead balls to create a crude 'dum-dum' bullet. A special local weapon was the vaulting-pole with a pike tip, which allowed men to scout and raid rapidly and aggressively across ditches and streams by pole-vaulting. Several Spanish units also seem to have copied this weapon and tactic.

Women sutlers could be found following every army; many were the wives of soldiers, and would sometimes even join their husbands in the ranks. Others would make a living by selling food, alcohol and other necessities, or their own bodies. Disease usually killed more men than fighting, especially during sieges, and syphilis (or 'Spanish pox', as the Dutch called it) ranked high on the list. Nevertheless, it can be argued that prostitutes did contribute to good order, by keeping the men inside their camps instead of causing mayhem in surrounding villages. The tolerated middle ground between the demands of Christian morality and of military morale seems to have been around five prostitutes per company. (Van Breen after Van Mander, early 1600s; RM)

WAR FOR INDEPENDENCE, 1588–1620

William Louis, Count of Nassau-Dillenburg (1560–1620), portrayed in his early thirties. He was 'the other stead-holder': each province had its own lord steward, but at various dates during the war these functions were combined in the persons of fewer individuals: at first William Louis in Groningen and Friesland, Maurice in the other provinces. William Louis grew up and was educated with his cousin Maurice and brother John, with whom he worked to develop the new-model army. He was the author of a famous letter to Maurice in 1594 that first described and illustrated the infantry 'caracole' by ranks of shot. In the same letter he provided Maurice with Dutch translations of the drill commands he had found in a work by the early 2nd-century Graeco-Roman author Aelian. Maurice went on to use most of these, and translated them into several languages. (Anonymous, c. 1600; RM)

Drill, training and supervision

Finding their inspiration in the study of the classical authors, and finally commanding all the rebel forces, Maurice of Nassau and his cousins William Louis and John continued their search for an effective army. At each court new ideas were first tested on the table, with lead model soldiers, then tried out with real soldiers. The desire to emulate the classics, and to create structure where vagueness had ruled, resulted in the famous training manuals of De Gheyn and Van Breen. These manuals were only meant to train recruits to go through all the same necessary steps (De Gheyn mentions that he has left out all the 'playful' unnecessary additions). Even more important was the introduction of a fixed set of verbal commands for a fixed set of actions. By this means men could follow orders quickly, with everyone knowing what to do, where to go, at what pace, and what to expect. Commanders and troops could now give and follow orders without hesitation, automatically.

It took a while for the troops (and the onlookers) to get used to all this marching around, which was quickly dubbed '*drillen*' ('turning around in circles'). Commands consisted of two parts: the preparatory order, and the executive order. More than 400 years later some of the exact same commands are still in use in the Dutch army, for example '*Rechtsom keert*' ('About face'). On a 'march' command, soldiers had to step off with their left foot (right if moving backwards). The pace was set by the drummers, who could beat a slow march, a quick march, a charge or a retreat. Drill in unison, two-part commands, fixed pace and men starting with the same foot: all these combined meant a unit would manoeuvre in step, and everything should tick like clockwork. It was perhaps not explicitly realized then (and is still overlooked by the majority of historians) that drill also increases a unit's morale and steadfastness, creating *esprit de corps*. These are exactly the qualities needed to field smaller, shallower and more isolated units successfully.

Planned or not, Maurice took full advantage of these new attributes. The new drill and organization meant that he could field three tactical units with the same number of men that his opponents concentrated in one. The troops had to practise all the time, even during the winter and on the march. This included firing practice; for example, at least once a fortnight groups of 20 to 30 men had to fire a minimum of four shots at man-shaped targets (muskets at a greater distance than calivers). Once a year every ten to 15 groups would compete for prizes (and punishment for those who still made basic errors, like failing to hit the target, or walking around dangerously with the barrel not pointing upwards). Officers had to study for tests too, requiring perfect scores; examples of these tests might be 'First question: 20,000 foot and 5,000 horse – How much does it cost to pay them for one month?'; or 'How many hours does it take them to throw up a rampart around their camp?'

At some time during the early 1590s regimental and army exercises were added, even wargames between opposing 'armies'. This allowed commanders to gain experience and men to get used to large-scale manoeuvres. Army exercises had another advantage: the preliminary inspections enabled the government to discover fraud more easily. It was hard enough to ensure that enough money was available to pay the whole army, and trickier to determine whether each company received pay for its real strength and not the usually higher 'paper strength'. After one such early surprise roll-call near Zelhem during a march to Grol (Groenlo) in July 1595, 1,000 absent men were struck off the payroll. Such precautions, together with regular payment (every seven, later every six weeks), and year-round employment, made sure that companies stayed much closer to their paper strength and that experience was preserved. During the early days William Louis tested most new ideas on the Friesland Regiment, which became the best-drilled and most up-to-date corps. Maurice was hesitant to risk it in open battle until the rest of his standing army had caught up, by 1597.

Less often illustrated than pikemen and musketeers, this is one of Maurice's 'targeteers' (from 'targe', a round shield). Men armed with sword and buckler were quite common in most armies of the 16th century, to defend commanders and ensigns and to break into pike blocks, and in 1580 each Dutch company was to have six of them. He wears breast-and-back plates with faulds to protect the belly, and note the hook at his right hip (see also page 44). The buckler was shotproof, so heavy and eventually unpopular; ceremonial bucklers were much lighter, and Maurice kept them longest in the guard of his army. He also devised a special version to be used during sieges: it had a vision slit to allow peeping over parapets without getting shot. His own life was saved by one of these shields during the siege of Groningen in 1594, when the English commander Francis Vere had a similar experience. Commanders would specifically request them during sieges, as the Count of Solms did at Hulst in 1595. (Van Breen, 1618; RM)

Formation of a 500-man division of four companies, in ten ranks; dimensions at right are in feet; dark shading = pike, pale shading = shot.
(Key:) C = colonel, H = captains, K = corporals, S = sergeants, V = ensigns with flags, L = lieutenants, T = drummers; M = second-in-command, usually lieutenant-colonel or sergeant-major, who would command a division if their regiment provided more than one. The division's commander and the captains would always be closest to the enemy, the lieutenants and second-in-command the furthest; officer seniority was from right to left. Each corporal was supported by a lance-corporal in the rear rank of his file. Any calivermen, as distinct from musketeers, would form the outermost files of the shot. In Maurice's time the first two ranks of pikemen were more heavily armoured than the other ranks. The drummers shown at the front would only be there if the division was operating alone. (Author's drawing)

Expensively inlaid private-purchase firearms of the early 17th century; while mechanically identical, normal issue muskets would not be decorated in this way.

TOP **Matchlock musket, early 1600s, about 5ft 3ins long (160cm).**

CENTRE **Wheellock from around 1625, 5ft long (150cm).** These and snaphaunces were expressly forbidden among the rank-and-file of the shot, though individual officers might own such expensive weapons. Note the long trigger guard, reminiscent of the old bar-trigger of the previous century.

BOTTOM **Matchlock musket of around 1625, just over 5ft long (154cm). (All photos RM)**

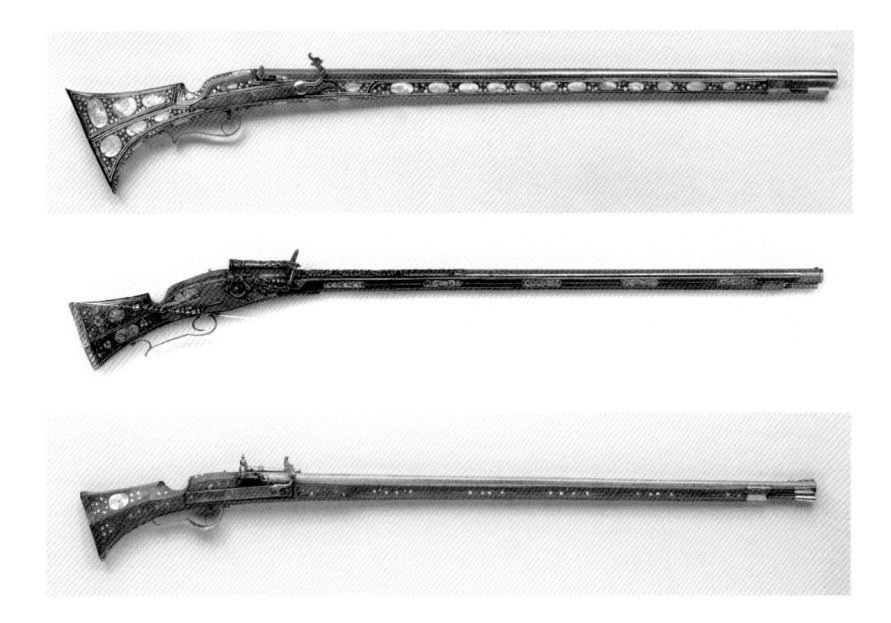

In a matter of a few years, all the plans and ideas had been tested and distilled into a set of most effective commands, drills and formations, which went on to deliver victory at Nieuwpoort (1600).

Organization

William's drive to reorganize and standardize continued under Maurice, to be finalized as state resolutions. As if to underline the reforms, the men now started to be called 'soldier' (*soldaat*), instead of the earlier 'servant' (*knecht*). As before, a company's cadre of officers consisted of a captain, two lieutenants, two sergeants, three corporals, two drummers, and – left in camp – a quartermaster and a barber-surgeon. Companies with more than 150 men also had a fifer, exchanged for a provost in 1599; so-called double companies – usually colonel's companies, and not always actually twice as big – had an extra sergeant. Besides these officers, a 150-strong company in 1589 had 39 pikemen (always the tallest men in the unit), ten halberdiers, three sword-and-buckler men/cadets, 30 musketeers, 52 calivermen, and three boys. Accepting the realities of life in the field, one of the soldiers would be appointed as a sutler. New recruits were trained by the corporals, and the eldest cadet was responsible for the company's arms and armour.

Within a decade halberdiers had disappeared from the regulations, and by 1597 companies had been equally divided between pike and shot. Twelve years later the caliver was finally stricken from the official organization and started to be phased out. Many captains had preferred muskets over calivers long before that, but they were forced to employ them, perhaps because the caliver's lighter weight and higher rate of fire made it better suited to operate on the flanks. Alongside the calivermen, most sword-and-buckler men also disappeared, although the bodyguards of dukes and princes might still be equipped with halberd or sword-and-buckler. (In 1596 the government suggested in vain that companies should be equipped with only a single type of weapon, retaining several mixed companies for garrison duties alone.) When calivers disappeared, a company's firearm-to-pike ratio also changed. From 1600 or so the ideal company had equal numbers of pikes, muskets and calivers, and when calivers disappeared the pike ratio in the company climbed from one-third to half, perhaps to better counter horse. In the early 1620s this ratio was made official.

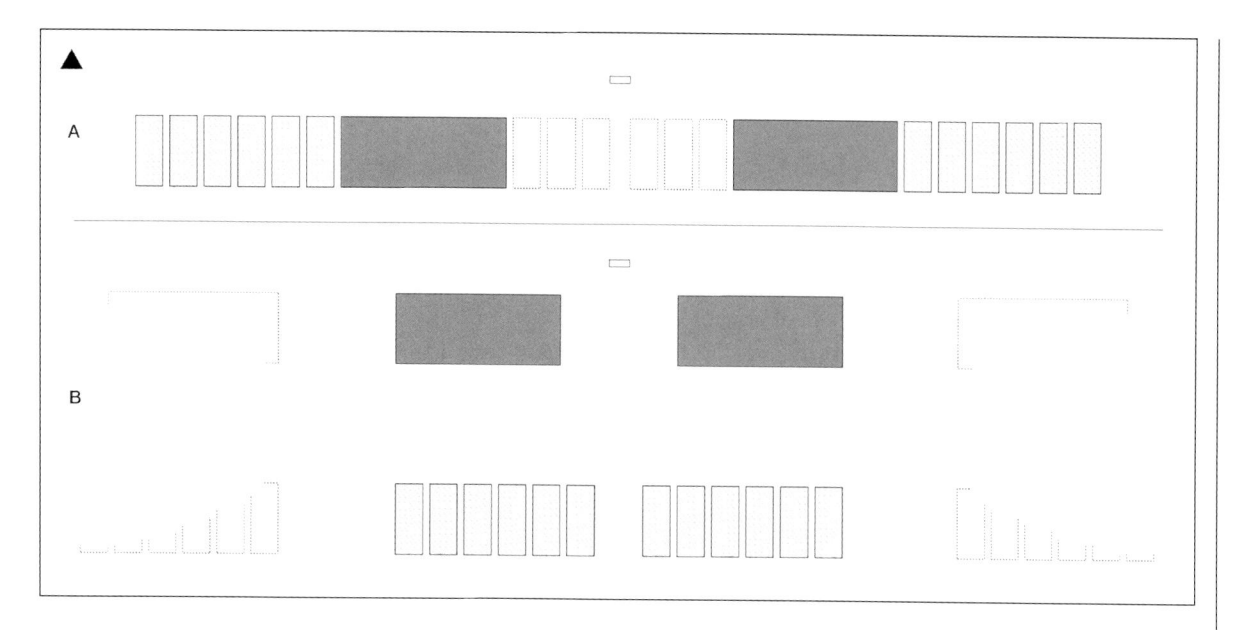

Regiments still did not have a fixed number of companies, but they did become administrative entities of their own, with their own colonel and a colonel's company. This latter was often larger and usually included quite a number of young noblemen, volunteering for a year or so to learn the trade while usually serving as ordinary pikemen. Regimental staff consisted of a lieutenant-colonel, a sergeant-major (who outranked captains), a drum major, and – left in camp – a quartermaster and a provost; a chaplain might also be present. During a campaign a government-appointed commissioner joined the regiment, to sniff out fraud and to keep a steady flow of recruits coming to make up for any losses. John van Oldenbarneveldt (1547–1619) was the country's 'grand pensionary', roughly comparable to a prime minister. It was he who ensured that the necessary bureaucracy ran smoothly, maintaining financial and political stability. In June 1604 Maurice explained to the government that an army could never be in the field longer than three to five months without losing up to a third of its number to disease and battle casualties.

Beyond regiments there were no fixed groupings, but John of Nassau-Siegen notes that in an army the ratio of foot to horse should be three to one. There were higher ranks than colonel, of course, up to the captain-general or commander-in-chief. Several deputies would always travel with each army, to report back to the government on a daily basis. In 1596 it was decided to increase the standing army to 12,000 men. This included the first foreign regiments in permanent service: one English (Francis Vere), one Scottish (Alexander Murray), one German to be formed from all the Germans in other companies (in 1599 under Ernst Casimir), and one new French regiment (in 1599 under Odet de la Noue). No doubt drilling became more effective once soldiers were put together according to their mother tongue: command leaflets were printed in Dutch, English, French, German and Scottish. When Maurice took over in 1588

A 1,000-man pair of divisions, in (A) the earlier wide formation, 450ft wide (137m), and (B) the later deep formation, only 200ft wide (60m). Dark shading = pikes, pale shading = muskets, white = vacated positions.

(A) Half the musketeers of each division, originally in the central gap, have moved out left and right to join those on the outside flank of their own pike block; however, at this date the pike blocks maintain the 100ft (30m) central gap, which was vunerable.

(B) This shows how Maurice solved the wide formation's weakness against cavalry, by concentrating the muskets behind the pike blocks, and closing the central gap to 50ft (15m). This allowed higher densities of men in both pike and musket units, and the musketeers were better protected by the pikes.

The formation's leader, usually a colonel, would be on horseback and have several drummers with him (small block at front centre), and – if this formation comprised the whole regiment – the regimental banner or colonel's ensign. (Author's drawing)

the whole army had 129 foot companies or 19,000 men. In 1600 it counted 264 foot companies, or 35,000 men. By 1607 that had increased to 353 foot companies, or 55,000 men.

In the field

Maurice fielded three tactical units for the 'manpower price' of one former unit. Maximizing the use of his expensive manpower, he made units shallower: ten ranks was the new norm, not the 30 ranks still common elsewhere in the early 1600s. He formed the men from the inactive rear ranks into new units, extending the line. A 1584 pamphlet stated that a unit would anyway collapse in rout after it had lost its front three to four ranks; indeed, the first experiments were done with five ranks only, and in his notes John of Nassau-Siegen mentions that the only reason to add another four or five ranks is because 'you have plenty of people'.

During deployment ranks were 6–7ft (180–210cm) apart and files either 3ft (90cm) or 6–7ft. During battle, ranks and files would close up to 3ft intervals. If things got really bad, pikemen would close both ranks and files up to only 18ins (45cm), but then they would not be able to turn. These distances were measured by holding out arms or weapons. Each man had a fixed position in the formation, so no matter the disorder the unit could quickly reform. On the battlefield, several companies were now combined to create – ideally – a 500-strong division, initially called a 'troop'; the surplus men too few to make an extra file were posted behind it. A division would deploy in the traditional way of a block of pikes (with its banners in the centre) with – at around 10ft (3m) distance – two flanks ('sleeves') of firearms, with the muskets closest in and the calivers on the outside.

For battle, two divisions would be deployed next to each other in a pair. The shot between the two pike blocks would then move out to join those on the outside flanks, but initially the pike blocks would keep their original interval of about 100ft (30m). Two or more division-pairs would form a brigade, with any unpaired division left acting as a reserve. During the march, units would split into (usually) four parts: firearms at front and rear, both pike parts in the middle, each of the same width and always ten ranks deep. If a column of march was formed by a single company, each of these parts might have anything from two to seven files; if it was a larger formation, then each part might be up to 50 files. On the field these four parts would form up to the left: i.e. the first halted, then the others lined up on its left side, forming a division or pair of divisions. Because each part was always the depth required for battle, they could quickly deploy into battle formation.

Three brigades formed an army, being called respectively the 'advance guard', the 'battle' and the 'rearguard'. On the march, brigades took turns marching at the head, as did the divisions within each brigade. On the battlefield, each brigade would form one line, so the army deployed in three supporting lines, with divisions or division-pairs in a chequerboard formation. Experienced commanders could and would adapt to particular situations. For example, in 1602 during the siege of Ostend, Francis Vere ordered his men, defending a wide breach against a 2,000-strong Italian assault, to fall and lie prone just as the enemy was about to shoot. After the Italian volley Vere's men quickly rose up, unharmed, to fight off the attackers.

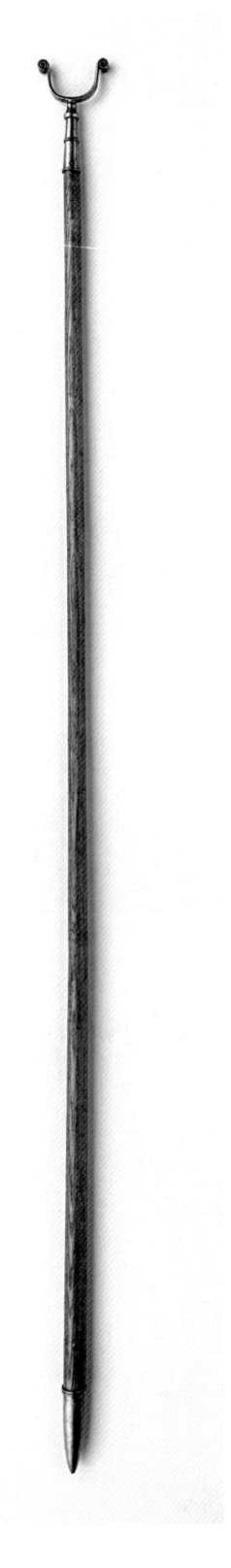

Musket rest, first half of the 17th century, 5ft (150cm) long. (RM)

John of Nassau-Siegen also had some non-regulation ideas. A general should ride a horse, never go in front of his units, and never join a unit, otherwise he would lose his overview of the whole. When a mêlée was inevitable, two ranks of musketeers should be put in front of the pikemen. These should hold their fire until the opponents charged, and after their volley they should either kneel under or retire through the pikes. Other important tips in John's notes are that it is always best to attack slowly and purposefully, and that units should never change direction during an attack.

Sometime after Nieuwpoort, Maurice made two important changes to improve the army's steadfastness and flexibility. Brigades would now deploy from right to left, so the first one to arrive on the field would take up a position with its division-pairs one behind the other, then the next brigade would march to extend these three lines to the left, and so on. This improved command and control, and immediately created depth the better to counter cavalry. Scaling this down, divisions and thus division-pairs likewise changed from wide to deep formation. The muskets were now posted 50ft (15m) behind their pikes, with ranks marching out to the sides to shoot in turn between the blocks. This allowed the two pike blocks to stand closer together, also around 50ft. Maurice designed this formation to overcome the shallower infantry formation's weakness against cavalry. According to his half-brother John, musketeers could now feel safe behind their pikes and focus more on their job (which was, according to John, to shoot at pikemen and officers, not musketeers). Moreover, the pikemen would no longer be disordered by musketeers running for cover during a cavalry charge (which cost the Spanish dearly at Nieuwpoort and Xanten); and the two pike blocks now stood close enough together to discourage enemy horse from advancing through the gap – if they tried, they would soon receive a deadly fire in both flanks, instead of riding down fleeing musketeers.

Another big advantage of the new method was that divisions and division-pairs could now be grouped in threes, without the need to adapt a division's individual deployment to the situation (as was still necessary at Nieuwpoort). This turned the previously 'odd-man-out' division extra to a division-pair into an integral part of a deployment, with brigades often formed up as a wedge (see diagram on page 35). Within the same brigade, divisions would be deployed 50ft (15m) apart, or with a gap still wide enough to allow a division to march through. Brigades would be 200–300ft (60–90m) apart laterally; the first line was 200–300ft in front of the second line, the third line 400–600ft (120–180m) behind it. All these numbers and formations were personally penned by the men at the top of the chain of command, such as Frederick Henry and Simon Stevin.

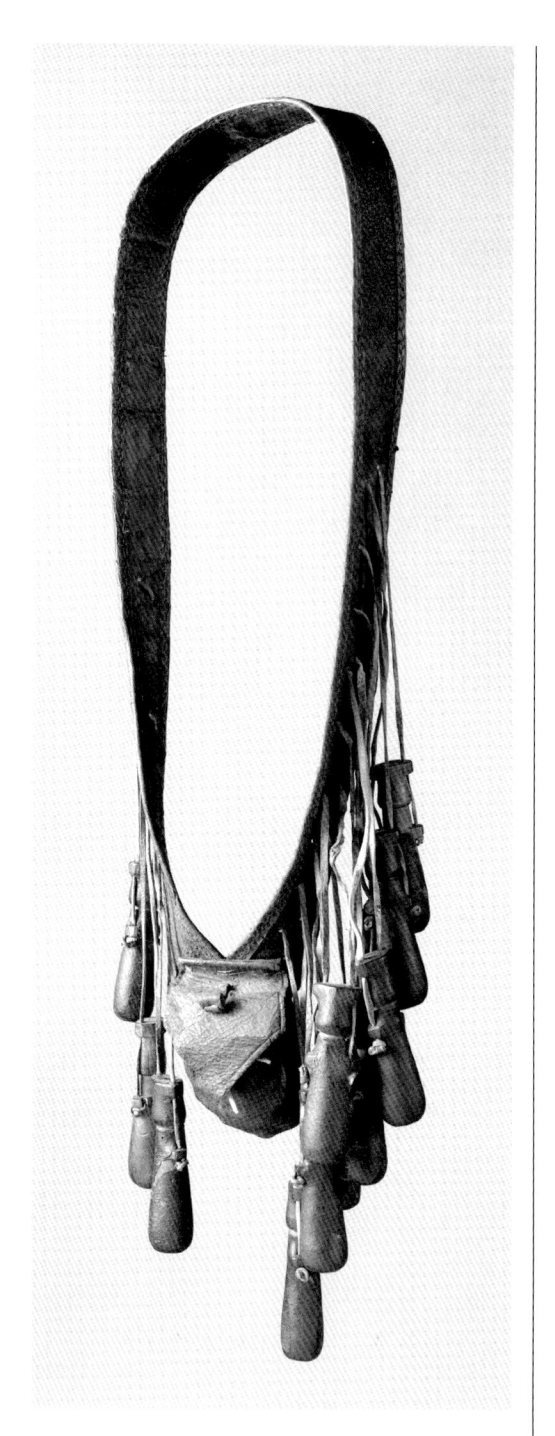

Musketeer's bandoleer with 'the 12 apostles' and a bullet-bag, first half of the 17th century. (RM)

Maurice practised and showed off these deployments – and the speed with which his drilled army could achieve them – at every opportunity when an enemy army was near enough to be discouraged by the sight (e.g. Gulik, Rees).

Combat drill

Maurice drilled his men not only to deploy in certain formations, but also to fight as a single entity, on command, without losing control. His units could thus continue to fire with the same efficiency as in the first volley. William Louis pointed out that a big problem of the old system was that units lost cohesion because calivermen would fan out in a screen, shooting from behind any kind of cover.

John's notes explain the drill in great detail. First for the pikemen: when cavalry were near they should close up, the first five ranks lowering their pikes with the butt against their foot. If fighting foot, they should hold their pikes horizontally and advance forcefully. When threatened on several sides, the five files on each side should turn to face the threat and lower their pikes.

John's notes on firearms are more extensive, and show the many modes of fire that the United Provinces' foot had mastered. In small units, if the men had to pass through their unit they would simply walk between the files. In larger units, e.g. a division, each firearms 'sleeve' would be divided into three or four sub-groups each led by a corporal. Each of these would close up their files to their flank file, forming pathways no wider than 6–7ft (180–210cm) wide between each sub-group. Now, if the men had to pass through their unit, each rank of each sub-group would file along these pathways, thus increasing the speed and decreasing the chance of disorder. Forming these sub-groups was usually done immediately after the first volley by the front rank. In a deep division-pair, files would close up into the gap between the divisions.

(1) Skirmishing. One or all files of a sub-group would advance about ten paces in front of the unit, angling towards its centreline. At the designated spot, the front man/rank would fire, turn and fall back past the others. The next would then step up, and so on. The cycle could repeat, or move along the line, and could be executed on several sides. This looping around was identical to the procedure used for firing practice (the '*kranendans*' or crane dance). This skirmishing by sub-group was the precursor of later platoon fire, in which the whole sub-group fired as one instead of rank by rank.

(2) Skirmishing Advance, either by rank or by file. If by file, the outermost file halts, quarter-turns and fires, while the next file starts the same cycle. After that next file fires, the first file moves adjacent to it; the two then do the same with the next pair, until all files are back in formation. If by rank, the front rank would wheel, then after firing each man would start to walk back the moment the unit had advanced past him.

(3) By Rank. When advancing, the next rank would pass the one that had just fired. When halting or in melée, each man would walk back through the formation, while his file moved up one position. A stationary unit could similarly fire to one or both flanks, using ranks as files. If cover was present, the ranks would 'cycle' up to it, then back again. If the unit was retreating – facing away from the enemy – the rear rank would halt,

quarter-turn, shoot, then pass through the unit to become the new front rank.

(4) By Unit. The unit would halt, the firearms would open files to 6–7ft and fire along the lanes between files, either by rank in quick succession starting with the rear rank, or all men together. In case of a threat from flank or rear, the men would first turn to face it and then open ranks to create the firing lanes. If threatened on several sides, the five files on each side would do so.

(5) Square. The firearms take shelter under the pikes, except for the best among them, who take up positions in the unprotected corners, holding their fire until the very last moment.

The soldiers' equipment

There were no regulations regarding uniforms, but the province usually supplied units with their clothes, often referring to unmentioned colours and patterns. Units recruited together could be expected to look the same. Again, blue is the colour most often mentioned in government papers. These also show that English troops invariable arrived dressed in red, while in 1598 Swiss troops still wore their traditional outfits. Plumes continued to be popular, orange-and-white being the most frequently seen. Officers, especially the higher ranks, usually wore orange sashes around waist or right shoulder. Extra money was reserved to purchase clothes for fifers and drummers, and a banner for each company. Guard companies would look fancier – more elaborate collars, and the like.

Arms and armour were increasingly supplied from central stores, purchased nationally and internationally. Armour was blackened. The 1599 resolution states that pikemen were to be equipped with a sword, a gorget, a breast-and-back plate, a pike of at least 18ft (6m), and a helmet. One in four also had to have arm and leg protection, i.e. pauldrons fastened to their gorget and tassets to their breast plate.

Calivermen were now required to wear a helmet. Each was to have a sword, and a caliver with a bore of 20 bullets to the pound, but actually shooting balls weighing only 24 to the pound (lighter than several years earlier), which were able to wound at 600ft (180m). Wheellocks and snaphaunces (see below, 'Coalition War/ The soldiers' equipment') were expressly forbidden. Musketeers also had a sword and a helmet, plus a rest, and a musket with a bore of ten bullets to the pound, but shooting balls at 12 to the pound; from a 4-ft (120cm) barrel, these could wound at 800ft (240m). Not mentioned but of course expected were powder and/or priming flasks, bandoleers, etc., as described above.

Any halberdiers and sword-and-buckler men still present would have been equipped like pikemen. Stiff fines were meted out for not wearing regulation armour, or for shortening pike or musket – all popular methods of lightening the load. Until about 1615 bucklers continued to be made in Holland in small numbers, but were no longer shotproof. In the 1590s Maurice had experimented with larger than normal numbers of bucklers,

Maurice experimented with even bigger shields than shotproof bucklers. These swordsmen wore similar helmets and half-armour to the mounted pistoleers (*reiters*), and note that this man also has greaves to protect his shins. While they proved effective in mock fights against trained pike units in 1595, such soldiers were only deployed in Maurice's guard , and probably not for long: their heavy shotproof armour and 'Roman' shields must have quickly exhausted them in combat. Shields like this were made in The Hague until the late 1610s, but only of wood and leather, for ceremonial purposes. Maurice also experimented with pike-and-buckler men, but they too were not seen outside his 'laboratory'. (Van Breen, 1618; RM)

Frederick Henry, Prince of Orange, Count of Nassau (1584–1647), aged 40. In 1620 he succeeded his half-brother Maurice as captain-general and eventually as Stead-Holder of all the United Provinces. Like Maurice, he too preferred sieges to pitched battles, but he also specialized in making rapid marches to outmanoeuvre opponents; he is mostly remembered for the many cities that he took. Unlike Maurice, he worked hard to create a royal image for his family: court life in The Hague, new palaces and a huge art collection all built his international prestige. His grandson was William III, Stead-Holder, and King of England, Scotland and Ireland (1689-1702) in joint monarchy with his wife Mary Stuart, daughter of the deposed James II. The present King William-Alexander of the Netherlands traces his ancestry back to Frederick Henry. (Delff after Van Mierevelt, 1624; RM)

for both swordsmen and pikemen, and even with Roman-inspired rectangular shields carried by even more heavily armoured men. Although these last proved very effective for men breaking into pike blocks – as witnessed during 1595 army exercises – they only saw service for a short while in Maurice's own guard. The general culture was one of simplification and standardization: eventually, only pikes and muskets would survive.

One last piece of equipment, and yet another way to protect the foot against enemy horse, was the *cheval-de-frise*, (interconnected) 6ft-long poles (180cm) with a metal spike, deployed in front of the firearms men. Though not always present, an army would certainly take them along for the initial phase of a siege, to use before ramparts were ready.

COALITION WAR, 1621-48

When the 12 Years' Truce ended, Spanish troops were already fighting in Germany in the meatgrinder that became the 30 Years' War, but the United Provinces were caught unprepared. There was no obvious threat to the economic heartland, and no financial plan. The morale of troops garrisoned in Germany along the border was low, because most of their officers were absent, fighting – and getting paid again – elsewhere. The government outlawed this, but also devised rules to manage the demand for officers and troops in Germany, France and Denmark. Nevertheless the problem remained in some remote areas (e.g. Roermond and Venlo in 1637).

Maurice died within a few years, his baton being taken by his half-bother Frederick Henry. The latter was less meticulous, more aggressive, and willing to form an alliance with France to take the fight to the enemy. As before, part of the army was 'standing' and part temporary. The wars in Germany and France meant that at times it was hard to find suitable recruits, while at other times unwanted and unruly veterans looking for employment flooded the country. Sometimes a whole foreign brigade or even army looking for employment was hired, either because of scarcity, or simply to prevent them being hired by the enemy. Sometimes penniless enemy units ripe for mutiny were 'recruited', to ensure that they stayed put and caused no problems.

Most troops recruited on a temporary basis by all the armies of these wars were unruly, since they were never paid on time. They plundered for the necessary means of survival, uncaring whether their victims were nominally allies or foes. Quite often these armies did not even see action, their mere existence being enough to deter the enemy's plans. As well as lacking discipline they were usually ill equipped and ravaged by disease. For example, in 1633 the States' cavalry was temporarily reinforced with 4,700 Swedish-Hessian horse; these behaved so badly, even by the low standards of the time, that despite many later offers no Hessian troops were ever again hired during the war.

At other times, however, when the troops were well provided for and drilled, great results were achieved. An example was a five-day march led by William II of Orange to besiege Hulst in 1645. Several rivers were successfully forded, and a battle was won, while the army feinted back and forth to confuse the enemy. Hulst was taken by surprise, several forts were stormed without delay, and strong enemy forces were unable to prevent the town being laid under siege.

(continued on page 33)

CIVIL WAR, 1568–87
1: Officer, 1572
2: Caliverman, c. 1577
3: 'Verrejager', 1574

WAR FOR INDEPENDENCE, c. 1600
1: Caliverman
2: Sergeant
3: Front-rank pikeman

WAR FOR INDEPENDENCE, c. 1600
1: Pikeman
2: Musketeer
3: Ensign

COALITION WAR, c. 1625–35
1: Musketeer
2: Pikeman
3: Officer

COALITION WAR, c. 1625–35
1: Dragoon
2: Musketeer for Swedish service
3: Skirmisher

FLAGS
See commentary text for details

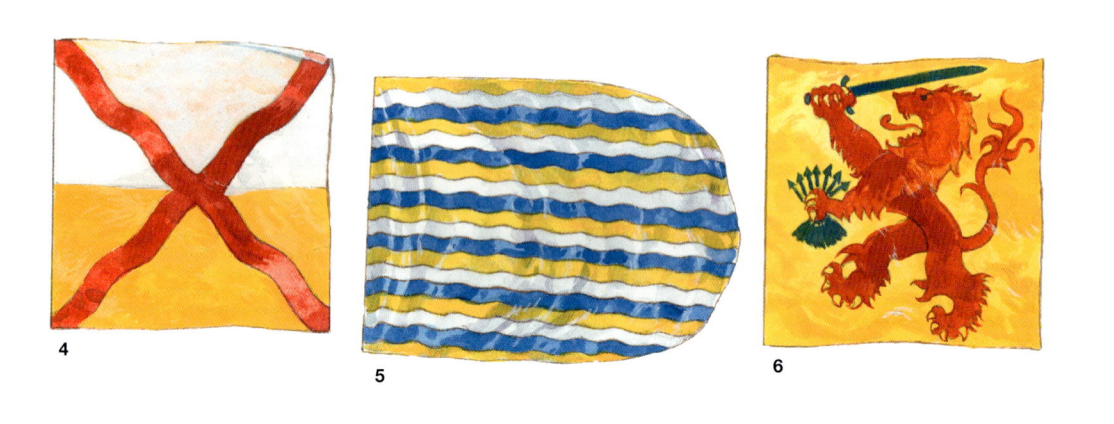

1

PRO · REGE · LEGE
ET · GREGE

2

3

· L · T · D · P ·

4

5

6

7

8

9

FLAGS
See commentary text for details

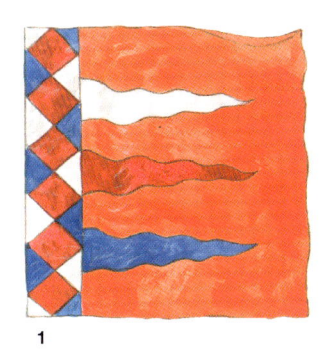

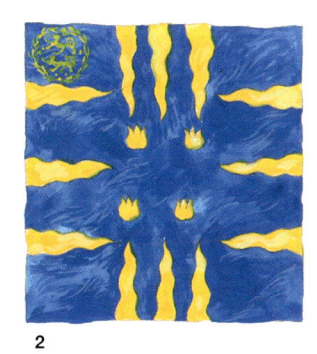

BRAZIL, c. 1640
1: European musketeer
2: Mulatto musketeer
3: Allied Tupi warrior

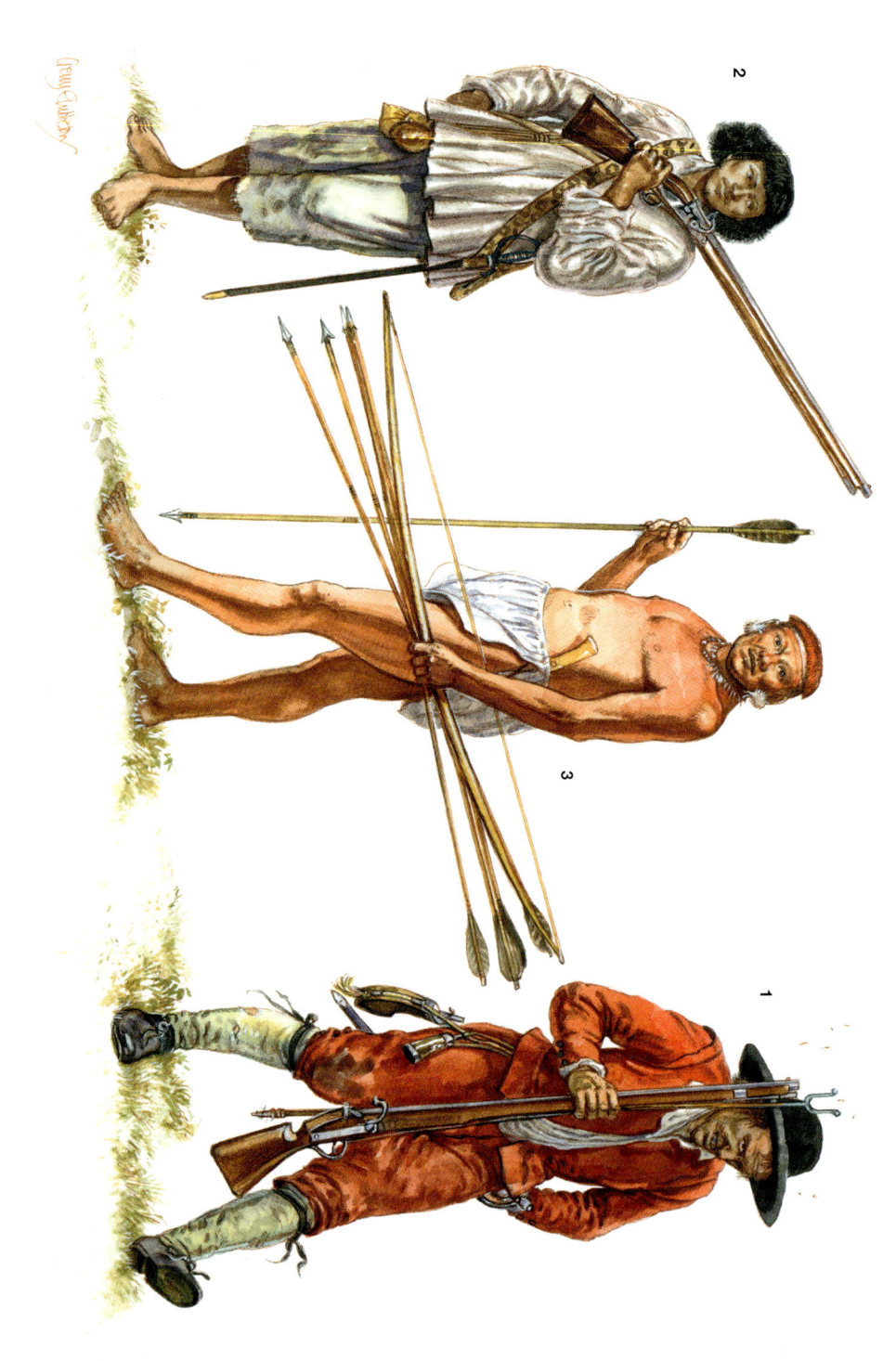

An aspect of this period was a new, speedy postal service that connected the army's field headquarters with the government. At 9pm every night, at each end of the line of communication a mounted courier would set off, taking 9½ hours to complete the journey between The Hague and Arnhem.

The army of Maurice and Frederick Henry also gained two extra important qualities from the mindset that develops from drilling. Firstly, it became an army of diggers, throwing up lines of circumvallation and contravallation to isolate cities in a matter of days; and secondly, it became an army of marchers, making full use of the interior lines of communication that it enjoyed in contrast to those of the Spanish.

Organization

Frederick Henry did not change the army's organization. Full-strength companies had between 100 and 200 men, with the same 13-man officer cadre as before, but a distinction started to be made between the higher and lower ranks. The captain, lieutenant and ensign were called officers, while sergeants, corporals and the others were called *onderofficier* ('underofficer'), as they still are today. The pike-to-musket ratio was firmly established as one-to-one. Maurice's last effort was the introduction of the flintlock to the army (see below); at first these equipped special flintlock-only companies, later a whole regiment. During the 1640s flintlocks started to enter service in the same numbers as the musket had done 50 years earlier: around one in every five firearms. These weapons were used by skirmishers guarding the flanks.

There were several other distinctive units as well. At the siege of Bergen op Zoom (1622) the Swiss company of Capt Walsdorffer fought

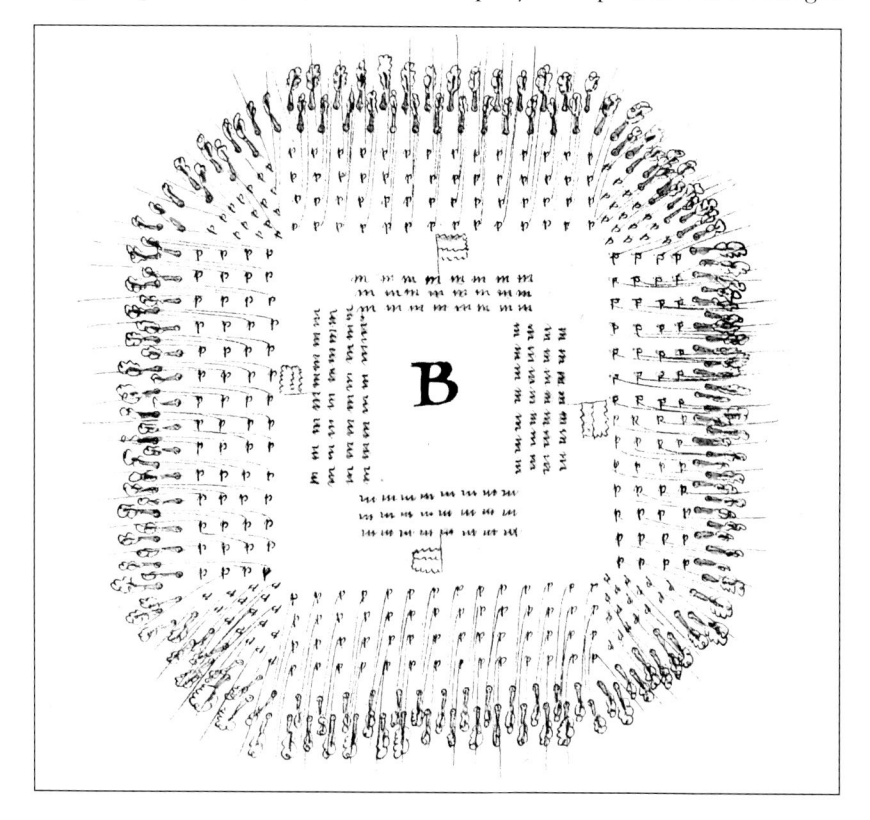

The field telescope was a Dutch wartime invention, and was demonstrated in 1608 to Maurice; magnifying by three times, the first examples probably entered Dutch service during the 12 Years' Truce. Hans Lipperhey tried to patent his invention in 1608, but the application was denied because many similar devices were already available. He should have tried instead to patent the diaphragm which he had designed and added to the magnifying tubes used by 'natural scientists'; this gave a much clearer and more focused image. (Detail, Van Berckenrode after Van de Venne, 1629; RM)

A diagram from the personal manual of Frederick Henry, handwritten during the 1610s and 1620s. It shows a four-company division drawn up in open square to receive cavalry. Note that all around the formation two staggered front ranks of shot shelter among the shafts of the first few ranks of pikemen. (KV A14-IX-2).

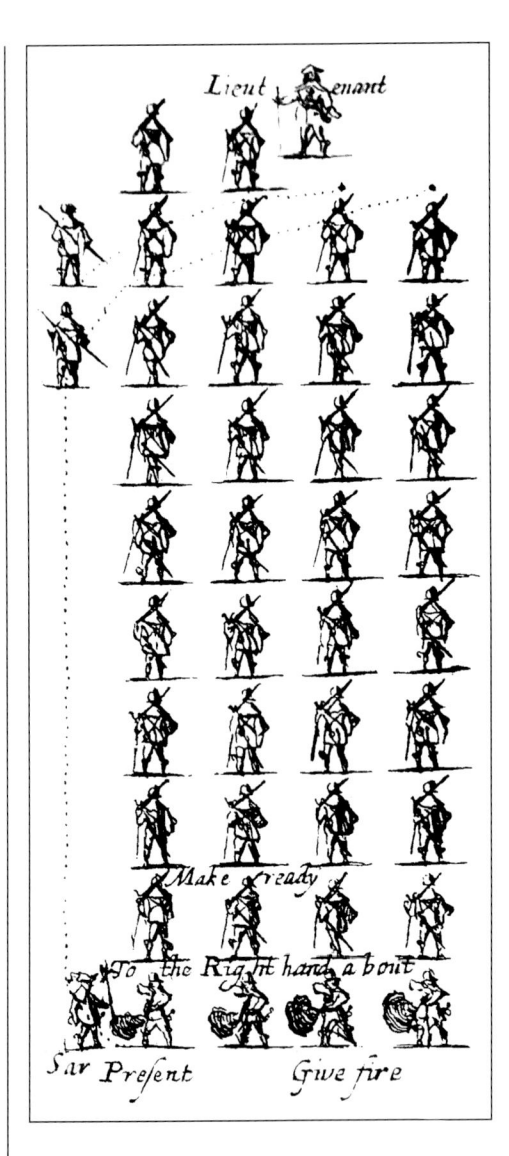

Detail from Henry Hexham's *Principles of the Art Military* (1642). After having served in the States' Army for many years, and choosing to stay instead of returning to England, Hexham published this military manual full of diagrams and examples, and followed it with a Dutch translation in the same year. This figure shows the firing drill of the left flank of a retreating company, giving fire under the orders of a sergeant by successive ranks, which then move (upwards – dotted line) to the front of the retreating unit – note the position of the lieutenant, furthest from the enemy. (KB)

off an assault equipped solely with two-handed swords (the captain did not survive). Because Maurice, like his father, continued to be the target of Spanish assassination attempts, the government wanted to pay for a unit of 40 Dutch carabineer bodyguards to provide round-the-clock protection, and to add a horse troop to his existing guard, but the captain-general refused this.

The majority of units were now contracted as complete regiments. The growing importance of the regiment as a tactical unit is also shown by the formation of the Guards Regiment in 1643. Although it had been called a regiment for decades, its companies had been officially independent and were merely deployed together; even though it was the most junior regiment of the army by date, its companies were the most senior.

Armies grew in size and in number. The 1631 army for the planned attack on Dunkirk had 200 foot companies. The Dutch-French army commanded by Frederick Henry in 1635 had around 45,000 foot and 8,000 horse. (However, both countries decided that this concentration was too much of a logistical challenge, and from 1636 the two armies again operated independently, supporting each other with detached contingents if necessary.) In 1647 the army's size for the peace that would soon come was planned to include 469 foot companies.

In the field

Until the end of the war, the army continued to deploy its divisions in the two standard formations: with the musketeers either as 'sleeves' on the flanks of the pikes, or as one group behind them. Frederick Henry marched his army around much more than Maurice had; he went south more often, where river transport was not available, so carts were regularly used to carry foot troops. If the main army went across the border one or two smaller armies would stay behind to defend against the inevitable counter-manoeuvre.

During the 1630s a new concept appeared: the flying brigade. This consisted of several companies of horse, usually harquebusiers, accompanied by at least an equal number of flintlock-men on foot or in carts, and it achieved some notable successes (e.g. Wipperfurt, Molensteeg). Sometimes *ad hoc* task forces were created. In 1629 all regiments at the siege of 's Hertogenbosch were stripped of a single company to form an assembled force to march off and counter an invasion further north. During the siege of Breda in 1625–26 the army stayed in the field throughout the winter, for the first but not the last time.

Many foreign officers learned their trade in the armies of Maurice and Frederick Henry, and several shared their new knowledge in books published after they returned home. It is interesting to compare the drill that the English officers Henry Hexham and John Bingham published 30–40 years after John of Nassau-Siegen penned his notes, to see how

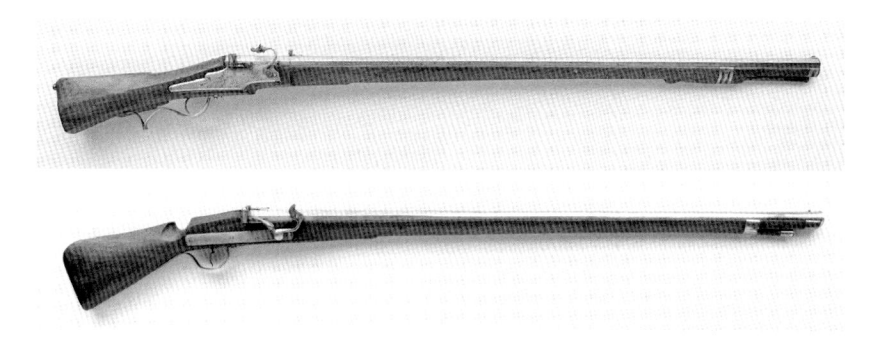

TOP **Matchlock musket dated to 1638, 5ft 6ins long (166cm). The old-fashioned extended trigger guard has almost disappeared.**

BOTTOM **Matchlock musket from the 1640s, 5ft 3½ins long (160cm). The 'modern' round trigger guard has now dispelled even the memory of the old trigger-bar of a century earlier. (RM)**

things had evolved since 1600. The formations and distances were generally the same, except that the pathways between the groups of musketeers were wider, 10ft (3m) instead of 6ft (180cm). While the musketeers were still deployed behind the pikes, the gap between the two had been reduced from the earlier 50ft (15m) to only 18ft (5m). The single-file skirmish drill had disappeared. Finally, single-rank firing had been supplemented by a sort of two-rank firing: the two staggered ranks walked forward together, fired in quick succession, then the next two ranks would repeat the procedure, and so on. It is not specifically mentioned that the flintlock companies were stationed on the flanks, but this is apparent from order-of-battle diagrams. The flintlock companies probably operated as skirmishers, introducing into the army the role of the later riflemen, *jagers* and *chasseurs*.

The soldiers' equipment

Men were perhaps dressed less uniformly than before, because payment – especially for temporary rather than 'standing' units – might be long delayed after actual recruitment. Orange sashes continued to be worn. With banners and sashes so prominent, both sides used each other's colours to deceive opponents during raids or when trying to take a town by surprise. Throughout the war ruses were much used, the most famous being Maurice's 'Trojan Horse', when men were hidden in a peat barge to capture Breda in 1590. Perhaps the most successful deception was

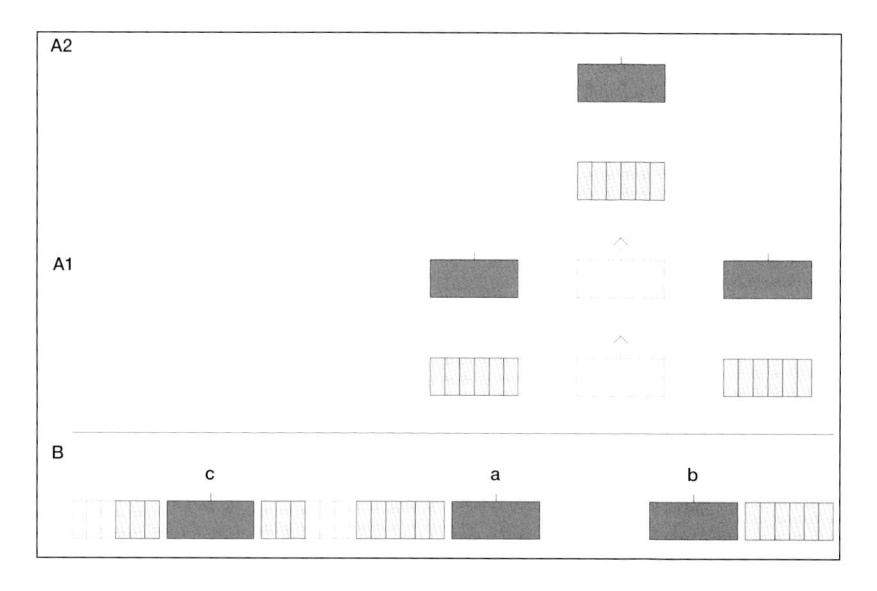

The early 17th-century change, to put the shot behind the pikes in 500-man divisions, made the need to form division-pairs superfluous; now every division had another within supporting distance. This in turn allowed 'odd-man-out' divisions to be used like any other, and increased the flexibility of the battle line.

(A1) Three-division brigade, c. 1605, deployed in line with shot concentrated behind pikes. Each gap between elements is 50ft (15m), each block 24 files or 75ft (23m) wide.

(A2) To shift into a tactically advantageous wedge, the central division simply advances. Any odd number of divisions could easily be deployed together, forming wedges all along the line of three, five or more divisions.

(B) The same brigade in 1600, using the original deployment of shot flanking the pike blocks. The two divisions on the right (a & b) have formed a pair, which leaves the left-hand division (c) as an 'odd-man-out'. The shot of this third division must either deploy on one flank of its pike block, leaving the other flank open; or – as here – must divide into two flanks. Since it should still preserve the prescribed distance from its neighbour, this complicates the brigade's deployment and manoeuvring – and even more so if the brigade wishes to form a wedge. (Author's drawing)

entirely unintentional, however. In 1627 the Spanish general Ambroglio di Spinola planned to invade Zeeland by surprise. His troops successfully crossed the water, and were preparing to storm the town of Goes when they saw a large number of banners marching along behind a dike they had to cross. Fearing that their surprise advance had been discovered, the Spanish invaders withdrew; but in fact the banners did not belong to a Dutch army, but to a crowd of happy peasants and villagers walking home after visiting the town fair.

Musketeers had their helmet, sword, musket, bandoleer, etc. as before. Pikemen now all wore the same armour: a gorget, breast-and-back plate, and tassets. As before, they were also equipped with a helmet, sword and 18ft (5m) pike. John of Nassau-Siegen distinguished three ways to carry the pike: the German, Spanish, and English. The German way was to lean it against the shoulder, point up and back, with the butt at knee level. The Spanish method was to balance it horizontally on one shoulder, and in the English manner it was held straight upright and tight against the body. John said that Maurice preferred the German way when manoeuvring on the battlefield, because it was less tiring than the other two, and made it just as easy to close up ranks and files as the English method.

After Maurice's death the army started to receive its arms and armour from national arsenals stocked with the products of national manufacture, which ensured speedy delivery and consistent standards. As a result inspections became more serious: instead of just earning a fine, muskets shooting bullets lighter than ten to the pound or with barrels shorter than 4ft (120cm) were now confiscated. Foreign regiments could, of course, enter service with 'the wrong' muskets, like the German regiment that left Danish service in 1629 to be snapped up by Frederick Henry: their muskets fired bullets of only 18 to the pound. As before, sergeants carried halberds, lieutenants and captains partisans. Captains were also required to carry a pistol, but only when on the march or on guard duty when they were without their partisans. Interestingly, during this period men were increasingly ordered to carry several days of rations with them.

During the last two decades of the war flintlock weapons started to enter regular service. The oldest snaphaunce (from Dutch '*snaphaan*', literally 'snap cock') surviving in Holland today dates from the 1570s, and many Scandinavian and Scottish recruits brought them to the Netherlands in the early 1600s. The snaphaunce

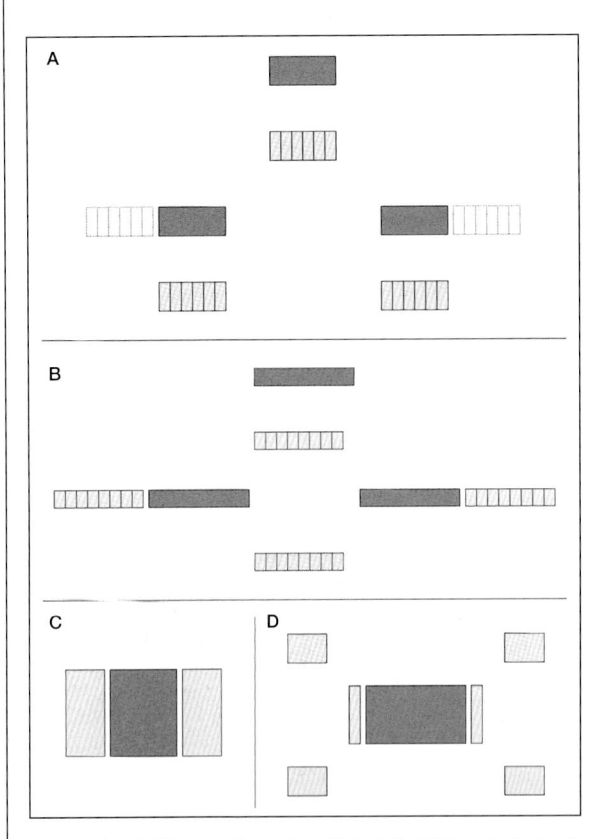

Comparing 1,500-man brigades: (A) Dutch, (B) Dutch-derived 1630s Swedish, (C) traditional German, and (D) Spanish. The Dutch, German and Spanish all had a pike-to-shot ratio of 1:1, the Swedes a ratio of 3:4, placing the surplus of firearms in the rear. The Dutch deployed in ten ranks, the Swedes in six, the Germans much deeper (here, 30), and the Spanish depending on the formation – here, a closed-up *square of ground* with ten ranks (a *square of men* would have several more ranks and fewer files). The Dutch formation is 375ft wide (115m), the Swedish 500ft wide (150m). Emulating the Swedes, the Dutch could fan out their firearms (in (A), white blocks), but it would be more efficient to add one more division to occupy the same frontage. Yet even with an extra 500 men, such a wedge, line or chequerboard of divisions would be more manoeuvrable and flexible than the Swedish brigade, which had the divisions much closer together, perhaps because they had fewer pike and shallower lines. Each Swedish division has eight 'platoons' (firing groups), and here each Dutch division six, but they too might instead use eight. (Author's drawing)

differed from the 'true flintlock' in that its frizzen or striker-plate was separate from the pan cover and freely movable by hand rather than their being a single spring-loaded assembly, and also in that it had no half-cock position. The Dutch arms industry took the step from snaphaunce to true flintlock during the 1630s, and surviving firearms from the 1640s are predominantly flintlocks. By then they were even exported to far-away markets such as the Iroquois in North America. The fact that a flintlock cost almost twice as much as the much simpler matchlock explains their slow spread amongst the often temporary, usually underpaid, and always expendable ordinary foot soldiers. Exact dates for the change are unknown, however, because both types of flintlock were popularly called '*snaphaan*', while the term for a skirmisher's weapon, '*vuurroer*', could mean either snaphaunce, flintlock or wheellock. In 1607 the first local unit was equipped with 'vuurroers'. These men also had a vaulting-spear enabling them to quickly cross the many ditches of the Betuwe country, during their mission to hunt down enemy plunderers and raiders.

In 1623 Maurice asked the government to raise four companies equipped likewise, and a year later the army already had ten 'vuurroer' companies. By 1632 two whole regiments had been added, each forming a flying brigade with several companies of carabineers. Such brigades performed the same function as dragoons in other armies. When the Guards Regiment was formed in 1643 one of the independent 'vuurroer' companies became part of it. By 1645 companies that had to man fieldworks each received 20 flintlocks for this purpose. Two years later four newly raised regiments each received 15 flintlocks per company, or 20 per cent of their firearms. At first no regulations covered the 'vuurroers', but in 1632 it was decided that they needed special bullets, of 18 to the pound, and the flintlocks destined for the troops in Brazil in 1647 were even lighter.

To alleviate temporary shortages of the professional soldiery, for example during unexpectedly challenging campaigns, civic guards and paid militias would replace professional garrisons in border cities. These were celebrated as important events in the cities that sent them, with commemorative publications, festive lists of everyone involved, etc. Here the Leiden civic guard marches to Grave in 1622, coincidentally across the Mookerheide battlefield of 1574. As shown here, at frequent intervals during the march they would be halted and drilled. Note the predominance of shot. (Liefrinck, 1622; RM)

HOME-DEFENCE & EXTERNAL OPERATIONS

John VII, Count of Nassau-Siegen (1561–1623), at the age of 54; in 1601–02 he had served as a field marshal in the army of the States' Protestant ally Sweden in its war against Poland. Raised with his brother William Louis and cousin Maurice, he too played an important role in the army reforms. Invaluably for historians, his many writings are still preserved; they include manuals, and a kind of flow-diagram for every level of command and every situation. Between 1596 and 1598 it was John who commissioned De Gheyn to make the plates illustrating the individual arms drills, and he founded the military college led by John Jacob von Walhausen (1580–1627). (Van de Passe, 1615; RM)

Civic guards

Cities had had their own burgher guards since medieval times, and many retained their old names throughout the war. Each unit was the size of a 'corporalship', perhaps 30 men. Later the bigger cities reorganized them on the basis of numbered districts. During the first decade of civil war they played an active part; with the power to open or close the gates to approaching rebels or royalists, they often decided which side the town would join. They saw little action except during sieges.

Besides the volunteer civic guard, from at least the 1570s there were paid militias ('*waardgelders*'). Most were organized by individual cities, recruited from among the poorest inhabitants. They were called up for a single campaign, to replace the garrisons of large frontier cities in Holland so that those professional soldiers could join the field army. In 1623, for example, 6,000 were recruited. They were not allowed to serve in their own city, however: e.g. in 1622 the Amsterdam militia had to go to Zwolle, and the Leiden militia to Grave. Individual garrisons might be as big as 40 companies, and in some cities one in every four men was a soldier. Paid militia were organized like the regular army, but without the camp officers. Every 12 days each company had to be drilled, and every two months as many companies as could be assembled had to exercise together. Their equipment followed the regulations for professionals. During the last decades the gorget seems to have become a sign of rank for militia and civic guard officers, who adopted buff coats in preference to plate corselets and tassets.

Fighting for allies

The foot troops of the States' Army did not only march into battle on home soil, nor did they comprise the whole infantry of the United Provinces. The Dutch received contributions of money and troops from other countries throughout the war against Spain, and they likewise supported their allies. At the start of the conflict Huguenots rode to the aid of the Nassau brothers, and the brothers marched to help them in France (e.g. Moncontour, 1569).

After the whole country rose in revolt, France and England each sent contingents. By 1600 most of these had been absorbed into the national army as English and French regiments. Returning the favour, nine Dutch companies joined Drake's and Norris's failed expedition to Corunna and Lisbon in April–June 1589 (the 'English Armada'). In 1599 some of the English regiments were sent back to England on two occasions, each time numbering around 2,000 men. In 1592 the French king was supported at Dieppe by 20 Dutch companies, including the guard companies. Two years later 22 foot companies and five cornets (cavalry squadrons) were sent overland to assist France against Spain, joined on the march by another 16 foot companies and four cornets. In 1595 three Dutch regiments were sent, and the United Provinces funded 3,000 new recruits in France; an extra 15 companies, led by Maurice himself, also briefly entered the fray at Calais. The following year another new regiment was financed.

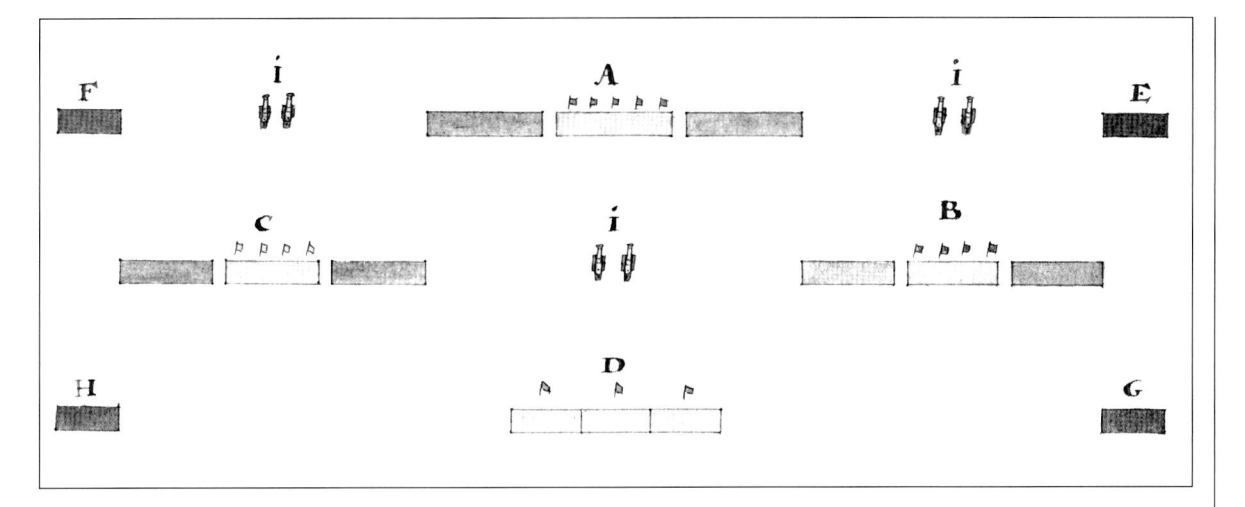

Protestant forces in Germany were supported with money, equipment and recruits, but also with interventions. In 1615 Frederick Henry took a peace-keeping force of the nation's entire horse and many musketeers to put an end to a conflict in Brunswick, and his imminent arrival quickly convinced the opponents to cease hostilities. In 1620 Frederick Henry marched into Germany again, now commanding 35 Dutch cornets and five guns, as well as 2,200 newly recruited English foot carried on 200 carts. He was supposed to join an army raised by Protestant princes, numbering around 12,000 foot and 4,000 horse, south of Frankfurt am Main. The princes had agreed that he would then take general command and seek out battle; however, when he arrived they refused to hand over their individual commands. The whole army remained passive, and the Dutch contingent returned home later that year.

The United Provinces also supported Venice in its war against the Pope and thus the Catholic League; from 1606 arms and training officers were sent, and in 1617 three specially recruited regiments arrived in Venice. These first participated in the siege of Gradisca, then served as marines in the Venetian fleet. A year later another regiment arrived, all veterans who had served under Maurice. The Dutch troops stayed until 1620.

Brazil and Angola

Economic advantage was an important war aim, and such gains could be achieved in faraway places that also needed protection, as far afield as South America and south-west Africa.

From the early 1600s Dutch merchants organized their seagoing enterprises into big share-holding companies, chief among them the West Indies Company (WIC) and United East Indies Company (VOC). If

Battle order for the expedition to take Luanda in Angola from Portugal in 1641; the force sailed from Brazil. Depicted are three wide divisions of pike and shot (A, B and C) totalling 13 companies; three companies of 'Brazilians' (D); six guns (i); and, at the corners, four flintlock companies (E, F, G and H), no doubt forming the skirmish screen. (Detail of the 1641 original: KV A04b-1454-148)

possible, local alliances were made, but the companies still needed land-based military forces to protect their trade interests and carve out monopolies. Most men were recruited in Europe, and sometimes these were used by the States' national army before being shipped overseas, as happened in 1629. The VOC army would grow into a large but scattered force, engaged all over Asia, but the biggest overseas army during this period was maintained by the WIC.

In New Amsterdam (today's New York) several small 'wars' were fought, but the majority of the manpower went to Brazil, where rivalry with Portugal (then in dynastic union with Spain) broke out into full-blown warfare in the first half of the 1620s, and again in 1630–41. In Brazil the Dutch made allies among local Indian tribes who rose against Portuguese rule, and these contributed large contingents to several battles (e.g. San Salvador de Bahia). A number of Indians were brought to Holland to learn the language so they could act as interpreters. Others sailed to Europe to be soldiers, serving as scouts in the States' field army; the last one retired some time around 1660. Many local Indians were recruited into the WIC army in Brazil, where they served alongside Europeans and mulattos (men of mixed race) as skirmishers. There were a few major clashes in Brazil (e.g. Porto Calvo and Guararapes, both twice), but most warfare was a guerrilla affair of exhausting patrols, long-distance raids and vicious ambushes. These men operated in small units and had to carry and haul along their own provisions. In 1631 the WIC army in Brazil counted 36 companies. The last force recruited to serve there was all of 6,000 strong, armed entirely with firearms; the first half arrived in 1648, the rest a year later, when the Portuguese victory in the second battle of Guararapes proved decisive.

These conflicts spilled across the South Atlantic to Angola, which was the origin of most of Portugal's slaves for their Brazilian sugar plantations. By 1624 an alliance had been concluded with a Congolese king to overthrow the Portuguese in Angola. In 1641, 20 companies and six guns landed to take Luanda, and after its capture 1,500 men were stationed there. These took part in several inland expeditions together with Congolese forces (e.g. Namboa Angongo and Kombi).

Throughout the period Europeans were dressed and equipped as per regulation, though it is not known whether the pikemen carried their full armour; musketeers seem to have left their helmets at home, preferring hats. Mulattos and other locals wore local clothes and used the same European weapons, but do not seem to have been employed as pikemen. The Indians' primary weapon was the bow and arrows; at home they went naked, but in the army they wore a simple loincloth. By 1640 flintlock-equipped companies had become an integral part of the WIC's Brazilian army, and four flintlock companies took part in the Luanda expedition in Angola. In 1648 the army received 1,000 flintlocks, shooting bullets of 20 to the pound from a 3½ft-long (105cm) barrel; the flintlock was, of course, much better suited to patrols and raids than the heavier matchlock. These men probably also carried a 6–8ft spear (180–240cm) instead of a sword, and had a cartridge bag instead of 'the 12 apostles'. Their companies had trumpeters instead of drummers, underlining their primary use as skirmishers.

REGIMENTAL GENEALOGY

The following panels include the regiments that *served for more than five years* in the pay of the United Provinces, listed by province or foreign origin, with their colonels' names and dates. Except where two or more colonels came from the same family, they are identified only by family name. *Note:* 'kia' means killed in action in the battle named; 'in the field' indicates a lieutenant-colonel or sergeant-major who led the regiment on campaign in place of an absent or elderly nominal colonel-proprietor. If a unit began as a colonelcy, the word 'formed' shows when it was taken into service by the States General as an official regiment. Of course, many more corps, regiments and independent companies also served, usually for only one or two campaigns (e.g. Mansfeld's 10,000-strong corps in 1622).

Guards:
(1) 1643 Gleser. The regiment included the formerly independent companies Prince's Guards, Friesland Guards, Groningen Guards (which had already been deployed together on the battlefield for decades) and Bouman's flintlock company.
 In 1572, the first unit of guards had been paid by the rebels to protect William of Orange; this was the traditional halberdier bodyguard of a stead-holder, drawing on much older origins. That unit was 'inherited' by Maurice, then by Frederick Henry, and finally absorbed into this new Guards Regiment.

Gelderland:
(2) 1576 Bossu, 1578 Steinbach, 1579 Hegeman, 1582 Berg, 1584 Turck, 1584 Nieuwenaar, 1589 vacant (in the field, 1589 Arent Brienen, kia Ostend), 1602 Lalaing, 1604 Heeckeren, 1607 Dorth, 1625 Varick, 1628 formed, 1639 Wolter Brienen, 1646 Dohna.

Holland:
(3) North Holland Regiment: 1572 Sonoy, 1578 formed, 1588 vacant, 1590 Dorp (kia Steenwijk), 1592 Duijvenvoorde, 1593 Frederick Henry of Nassau (in the field, Duijvenvoorde, kia Ostend), 1602 split into Zuijlen (and new Hornes), 1608 Dorp, 1628 Rijswijk, 1631 Hanau (kia Maastricht), 1632 Rijswijk again, 1636 Henry of Nassau. It suffered 80 per cent losses at Hardenberg in 1580.
(4) 1580 Thiant (kia Antwerp), 1583 Justinus of Nassau, 1585 Philip of Nassau, 1595 Egmond, 1609 decommissioned.
(5) 1586 Hornes, 1605 (in the field, Swieten), 1613 decommissioned.
(6) 1580 IJsselstijn, 1589 Brederode, 1599 vacant (in the field, Ghistelles, kia Ostend), 1604 vacant, 1623 Brederode.
(7) 1602 Charles, 1625 Hornes, 1625 Grenu, 1629 Solms, 1630 formed, 1641 Hornes.
(8) 1632 Pijnsen, 1637 vacant, 1640 Huygens (kia Gennep), 1640 Does. First '*vuurroer*' (flintlock) regiment.
(9) 1632 Rosencrants (kia Venlo), 1635 formed, 1635 Beverweerd.

Zeeland:
(10) 1572 Alexander Haultain, 1586 Sidney, 1587 Solms, 1596 Maurice of Nassau, split in three new colonelcies: Piron, Dorp and Noot; 1614 (in the field, Philip Haultain), 1627 William Haultain, 1637 vacant.

Utrecht:
(11) before 1584 Villers, 1586 Nieuwenaar, 1590 Groenevelt, 1599 Huchtenbroek (kia Ostend), 1601 Loon (kia Ostend), 1604 Utenhove, 1626 Dieden, 1628 formed, 1641 Brant, 1641 Renesse.

Friesland:
(12) 1577 Rennenberg, 1580 Hohenlohe, 1580 formed (in the field, Rummen), 1584 William Louis of Nassau (in the field, Sedlnitzky, 1591 Hettinga, 1603 Eijsinga), 1620 Ernst Casimir of Nassau (in the field, Eijsinga), 1631 split into Emminga (and new Roussel), 1635 Oenema, 1646 Schwartzenberg. In 1580 Rennenberg had switched sides and handed Groningen over to the royalists.
(13) 1631 Roussel, 1637 Aysma, 1637 Potter, 1637 Aylva.
(14) 1639 Schwartzenberg, 1647 Hettinga.

Overijssel:
(15) 1632 Wijnbergen. Second '*vuurroer*' (flintlock) regiment.
(16) 1647 Ittersum.

Groningen (aka Stad en Lande):
(17) 1594 William Louis of Nassau, 1620 Maurice of Nassau,1625 Ernst Casimir of Nassau, 1633 Eussum (who had been field commander from the start), 1639 Starkenborch, 1646 Isselmuden.
(18) 1647 Beyma, 1647 Gockinga.

Foreign – English:
(19) 1578 Norris (Noureys), 1587 Willoughby, 1589 Morgan,1590 Francis Vere, 1599 formed, 1605 Cecil, 1632 Packenham, 1635 Culpeper, 1640 Craven.
Between 1573 and 1584 Morgan tried several times to raise his own English regiment for Dutch service, but to no avail. Until 1599 part of the troops were in Dutch pay and part in English pay, but all under English authority. In 1589 those in English pay mutinied and handed over the city of Geertuidenberg to the royalists. In 1598–99 the force was reorganized, all in Dutch pay and solely under Dutch authority.
(20) 1599 Horatio Vere (in the field, 1605 Sutton, 1606 Meetkercken),1633 Goring, 1647 Killegrew.
(21) 1605 Ogle, 1622 Morgan, 1642 Cromwell.
(22) 1616 Sidney, 1623 Harwood (kia Maastricht), 1632 Herbert, 1644 Knightly, 1646 Aubrey Vere.

Scottish:
(23) 1573 Ormiston, 1574 Henry Balfour (who killed Ormiston in a duel), 1580 Preston (killed by his own men), 1583 Renton (Benton?), 1583 Boyd, 1584 Bartholomew Balfour, 1594 Murray (kia Bommel), 1595 formed, 1599 Edmond (kia Rijnberk), 1606 Brogg, 1635 Sandilands, 1639 Erskine.
(24) 1574 William Stewart of Houston, 1577 went to serve in Danzig, 1579 returned, 1583 merged with Preston (see above).
(25) 1604 Walter Scott of Buccleugh, 1612 Robert Henderson (kia Bergen op Zoom), 1622 Francis Henderson, 1628 Halkett (kia 's Hertogenbosch), 1629 David Balfour, 1639 Douglas, 1639 Kirkpatrick.
(26) 1629 Walter Scott of Buccleugh, 1633 Livingstone,1640 Philip Balfour, 1646 Drummond.

French:
(27) 1599 Noue (taken prisoner), 1600 Henri Coligny (kia Ostend), 1602 split into Leonidas Bethune (and Hallot), 1603 Gaspard Coligny (Marshal of France), 1638 Maurice Coligny, 1644 Gaspard Coligny, 1648 Hautcourt.
(28) 1602 Hallot (kia Muelheim), 1605 Syrius Bethune, 1613 St Simon (kia 's Hertogenbosch), 1629 Perponcher, 1645 Rechine.
(29) 1615 L'Aubespine.
(30) 1625 Nogaret, 1639 Fleury, 1641 D'Estrades.
(31) 1634 Charnace (kia Breda), 1637 Plessis.

German:
(32) 1599 Ernst Casimir of Nassau, 1625 formed, 1631 Henry Casimir of Nassau, 1641 John Albrecht of Solms, 1646 Henry Trajectinus of Solms.
(33) 1622 William of Nassau, 1642 Puechler.
(34) 1625 Hatzfeldt, 1625 Merwede, 1626 Neuhoff (kia Dessau), 1626 into Danish service; loaned to Mansfeld, destroyed at Dessau 25 April 1626.

Walloons:
(35) 1600 Frederick Henry of Nassau, 1602 Hertaing, 1606 John Ernst of Nassau-Siegen, 1617 Philip Levin Famars, 1627 William Levin Famars (kia 's Hertogenbosch), 1629 John Maurice of Nassau, 1644 William Frederick of Nassau. As the royalist garrison of a surrendered fort they had chosen to enter Dutch service, led in the field by Hertaing. They were then known for a while as 'new beggars', taunting their royalist ex-comrades by still wearing red sashes but over the left (wrong) shoulder.

Others, all decommissioned 1647:
(36) 1629 Thomas Ferentz.
(37) 1629 Loo, 1635 vacant, (in the field, Enno Ferentz),1640 Enno Ferentz.
(38) 1631 Walraven.
(39) 1631 Erentreyter.
(40) 1632 Henry of Berg (23 companies), 1634 formed (12 companies),1641 Frederick of Berg.

To be continued: *The forthcoming second volume MAA 513 will cover the cavalry, artillery, and engineers; it will examine how all branches worked together on the field of battle, and will include a chronology of sieges. It will conclude with remarks on the legacy of the army of Maurice of Nassau. The following selected list of source works applies to both volumes.*

SELECT BIBLIOGRAPHY

Hahlweg, W., *Die Heeresreform der Oranier, Das Kriegsbuch des Grafen Johann von Nassau-Siegen* (Wiesbaden, 1973)

McNeill, W.H., *Keeping Together in Time – Dance and Drill in Human History* (Cambridge, 1995)

Ten Raa, F.J.G., & F. De Bas, *Het Staatsche Leger 1568–1795*, Vols I–IV (Breda, 1911, 1913, 1915 & 1918)

't Hart, M., *The Dutch Wars of Independence: Warfare and Commerce in the Netherlands 1570–1680* (New York, 2014)

Van der Hoeven, M. (ed.), *Exercise of Arms – Warfare in the Netherlands 1568–1648* (Leiden, 1997)

Van Nimwegen, O., *The Dutch Army and the Military Revolutions, 1588–1699* (Suffolk, 2010)

PLATE COMMENTARIES

All the armour and most weapons depicted in the colour plates are on display in the National Military Museum. Regulations specified blackened armour. To prevent rust, the exterior of armour and the hilts of edged weapons could be blackened by applying a mixture of linseed oil and soot; after heating, this left a permanent black layer. Browning and blueing were more expensive methods; the cheapest and least effective was to simply paint the metal.

A: CIVIL WAR, 1568–87
A1: Officer, 1572
This officer of the first decade of the war wears a burgonet helmet with orange, white and blue plumes attached at the rear; and half-armour of a gorget, rerebraces on the upper arms, breast-and-back plates and knee-length cuisses, decorated by leaving some parts unblackened. He carries a sword and a so-called 'hunting' halberd – an officer's symbol of rank during the late 16th century, like the partisan. He is based on the 1572 portrait of Barthold Entens van Mentheda, an esquire from Groningen province. One of the many Protestants who had to flee for their lives, he came back with a vengeance as a much feared 'sea-beggar', terrorizing the northern waters and provinces. He was part of the fleet that landed at Den Briel, commanded the capture of Dordrecht shortly afterwards, and was engaged at Goes and second Manpad (Haarlem). After Stead-Holder Rennenberg and the city of Groningen switched sides, Entens and William Louis of Nassau (the new stead-holder for the rebels) commanded the force that laid siege to the city in 1580. Entens was killed there on 27 May, supposedly when he drunkenly charged the outer works and thrust his head into an embrasure just as its cannon was fired.

A2: Caliverman, c. 1577
A typical caliverman of the era; during this period the long trigger-bar was replaced by a short trigger, the bar shape being retained as a trigger guard. He wears the fashion of the time, including the neck-ruff collar, and his morion has been decorated with brass rosettes round the base. The colours are taken from the De Gortter manuscript, a series of contemporary sketches of dress and banners of the units based in Mechelen between 1577 and 1585. Most armour would have been imported from Germany or Italy.

A3: *'Verrejager'*, 1574
This 'far hunter' during the siege of Leiden is taken from an anonymous 16th-century painting in that city. The many ditches in the Dutch landscape limited the use of cavalry

Morion, second half of the 16th century; today popularly associated with Spanish troops, in fact this type of helmet was worn by infantry all over Europe and was widely manufactured in Italy. This example has an embossed 'lily' decoration left unblackened, and brass rosettes; note too the protective plates on the reconstructed leather chinstrap. (RM)

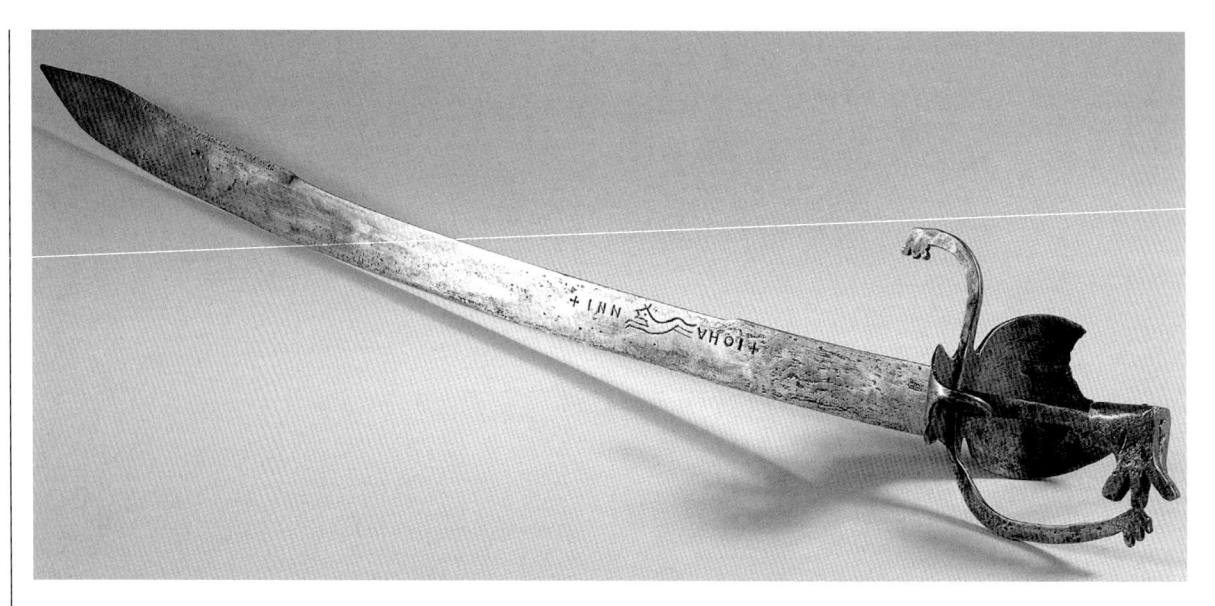

A common type of late 16th-century infantry sword, nowadays called a 'Sinclair sabre', although in fact it resembles a cutlass. Note the swordsmith's marks on the blade, and the crude workmanship of the basket guard. (RM)

and also hindered infantry formations. Many were too wide to simply leap across, but vaulting-poles allowed easy crossings (and are still in use today). A disc at the forward end prevented the tip from sinking too deeply into the mud, and adding a metal spike to the other end produced a sort of 'vaulting-spear', giving a man both high mobility and a vicious sting – ideal for raids, and when hunting down enemy raiders. Later the 'hunters' would also be equipped with a wheellock or flintlock, and served on the flanks or in cooperation with horse, much like dragoons in other armies. At Leiden and elsewhere they were also used as messengers, and to bring much-needed supplies into the city. This man wears civilian clothing with a white handkerchief tied around his arm as a field sign; since raids usually took place during dawn or dusk, quick identification of friend or foe was vital. A sheathed dagger shows under his shirt behind his hip.

B & C: WAR FOR INDEPENDENCE, c. 1600

While omitting a sword-and-buckler man (see page 17) this otherwise shows the ideal mix of troops for a company, as envisioned by Maurice of Nassau, written down in regulations, and seen on the field at Nieuwpoort.

The **caliverman (B1),** serving on the outer flank of the shot, has a weapon with a straighter stock than before. The **sergeant (B2)** would be as heavily armoured as the two front ranks of pikemen, with gorget, rerebraces, breast-and-back plates and tassets. Earning more than them, however, he would probably have more fashionable clothes, and is distinguished by an orange sash and lavish feather plumes. Another sign of his rank was the 8ft (240cm) halberd, in this case with a squared, grooved shaft with rounded-off corners, and two protective langets running down for about 19½in (50cm) below the head. The 18ft (5m) weapon carried by the **two front ranks of pikemen (B3)** had similar langets; its shaft was about ⅜in (1cm) thicker in the middle than at the ends. The helmet is the '*stormhoed*' ('storm hat'), recalling the old medieval 'kettle-hat', which offered good protection. Note that the gorget was always worn underneath the cuirass. The men's swords are simple and straight, meant for both hacking and stabbing.

Most **pikemen (C1)** in the body of the block did not have arm or leg armour. Unlike the caliverman, the **musketeer (C2)** serving in the inner flanking files carries his charges individually measured into the 'apostles' or cartridge-bottles strung from his bandoleer together with a bullet-bag and spare match, and has a forked musket rest. Various helmet designs were used in different units, since the arsenals still purchased throughout Europe. The unit's **ensign (C3)** would probably be a young nobleman, and thus wears clothes of finer quality, and in this case his armour is decorated with

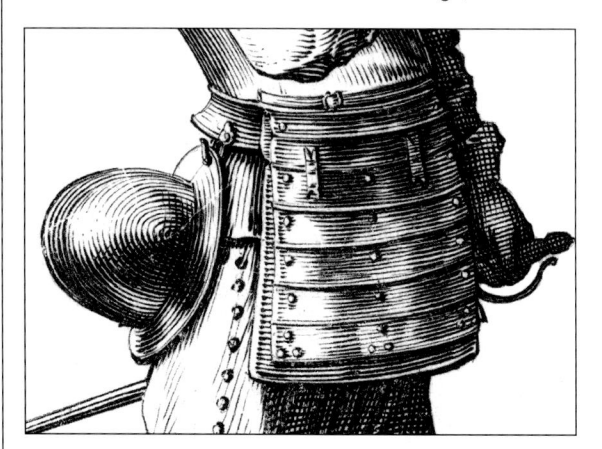

A pikeman's corselet might have a hook on which he could hang his helmet while on the march. No helmets have yet been found with a hole in the brim for this purpose, but the evidence of period prints is explicit. (Detail from a Savery print, 1630s; RM)

brass rivets and edges. He carries the national banner prescribed for all Dutch regiments in 1600 (see F6); the finial was a functional pikehead, and, characteristically, the staff exposed below the silk is only about 10ins (25cm) long, with an egg-shaped counterweight.

D & E: COALITION WAR, c. 1625–35

In Frederick Henry's army the troops' equipment became ever more standardized. Dutch factories were now mass-producing regulation equipment, and national arsenals were able to supply whole armies in a matter of days (e.g. Mansfeld's 10,000-strong corps in 1622). Helmets and armour were mechanically made, with water-powered hammers beating single plates into shape. The result was simple and cheap, of a quality perhaps not as good as some earlier products, but consistent.

Musketeers (D1) were still supposed to wear helmets, but it seems that most 'forgot' to bring them along. Their muskets had now developed the rounded-shape trigger guard still used today. All **pikemen (D2)** now wore the same armour: breast-and-back plates and tassets, over a heavy leather 'buff coat'. Although regulations called for blackened armour, some period paintings show it like this. The helmet was developing into the simple 'pikeman's pot'; losing the comb, it would soon degenerate further into the model that continued to be used for another century. **Officers (D3)** now seemed to prefer buff coats to the heavier half-armour worn in the previous decades, and carried a partisan as well as their sword (here belted at the waist, under the costly sash). Period engravings show the hat brim extravagantly flared up at the front, and officers in portraits wear very broad lace collars.

Dragoons (E1) were a short-lived experiment in Maurice's army. Infantry now and then hitched a ride with cavalry, like the 500 men who took Mons in 1572, or those who stole a march on the enemy in 1606 to occupy Bredevoort castle just in time. But it was not until 1606 that the States' Army decided to follow the foreign trend, and converted two foot companies into dragoons: Elderen (Capt Hoboken's old company of Ostend veterans, whose banner is shown in the De Gortter manuscript – see under F5), and Otmarson (the Scottish company of Col Sinclair, also Ostend veterans). These were most probably armed with a slung snaphaunce, already a popular weapon among Scots entering Dutch service; John of Nassau-Siegen said it was a prerequisite for dragoons. He also mentioned that they should not carry banners, and only a small drum. The companies had neither pikes nor armour, but Elderen (in Frisian pay) complemented their firearm with the vaulting-spear, to enjoy even more flexibility of movement. Apparently their horsemanship had improved enough by 1615 to convert both units into full horse, as carabineers. This ended the use of dragoons in the army, their function of mobile infantry being taken over by foot equipped with vaulting-spears.

Hardly any uniform colours are mentioned in period texts, but in 1629 men recruited in north-west Germany and the Netherlands to serve in Gustavus Adolphus' **Swedish army (E2)** were referred to as 'black clothed'. Before they left, Frederick Henry hired them to garrison some of the cities threatened by Montecuccoli's failed invasion (intended to relieve the siege of 's Hertogenbosch). These so-called 'Swedes' totalled 2,600 men in three regiments (Van

Typical felt hat of the first decades of the 17th century. This example, of a greyish-beige colour, belonged to the Stead-Holder of Friesland, Groningen and Drenthe, Ernst Casimir of Nassau-Dietz. He was wearing it when he was fatally shot through the head while peering over a parapet during the siege of Roermond on 2 July 1632. (RM)

Falkenberg, Dietrichson and Hall) of eight companies each, and served Frederick Henry from July until October 1629. Only the two companies garrisoning Amersfoort actually met Montecuccoli's troops.

The **'skirmisher' (E3)** is from the *'vuurroer'* company of the Guards Regiment in the 1640s. He is equipped with a flintlock and still uses a bandoleer, although cartridge-bags (as worn slung to his hip by E1) seem to have been introduced in flintlock units at about this date. The standing army had two regiments and several companies of flintlock skirmishers, who operated on the flanks, or – with carabineer horse – in independent flying brigades. Many if not most also had the vaulting-spear, or – where those were impractical – the 6–8ft-long (180–240cm) spear called a 'third pike' (because it was around one-third the length of a normal pike). It seems that the 1,000 musketeers detached in the 1620s to serve as marines in the navy had also received flintlocks by this later date.

F & G: FLAGS

As the army changed from a mercenary *Landsknecht*-type organization gathered for each campaign into a drilled standing army, so too did the unit flags (aka ensigns) carried by the troops develop. The old banners were carried on short pike-headed poles, used as weapons if need be, and were meant to convey regulated signals for movement orders (a practice that still survives as traditional flag-waving competitions around Europe). Companies lost their individuality in the new regiments, and the banner's visual messages were replaced with drill and voice commands. As a result the ensigns grew smaller, but the poles grew longer – or at least that was true of the leading banner, the colonel's ensign. This was carried apart from the company ensigns, which were all grouped together in the central pike block, officially between the third and fourth ranks. If regulations were followed the company flags were all pretty much identical, no doubt leading to some confusion on the march. Towards the end of the period only the regimental banner may have been retained, with companies using simple coloured flags to avoid confusion. This was certainly the case among the WIC troops, the regiments sent to Venice, and – still later – urban civic guards. The flags were renewed whenever necessary; some survived for as long as 16 years before a new captain or colonel decided to change them.

F1: William the Silent at the battle of Dalheim in 1568, based on descriptions and Hogenberg's print. His ensign bears the motto 'Pro . Rege . Lege / et . Grege' ('For King, Law / and People'), as used in his 1568 pamphlet calling on the people to resist Alva's Spaniards. Since the king himself represented order and authority, however, he was still considered to be on the 'good' side. At Heiligerlee, William's brother Louis used 'Nunc aut Nunquam' ('Now or Never'), and 'Recuperare aut Mori' ('Regain or Die').

F2: Captain Wolter Hegeman at the siege of Deventer, 1578, from a contemporary painting. Born in Harderwijk in 1542, he was banished by Alva in 1566, when his father was the city's burgomaster. He became a rebel, was a *hopman* (captain) by 1572, and colonel of the Gelderland Regiment by 1579. He died at the siege of Bronkhorst, shot by a deserter. Illustrating the chaotic nature of the early Civil War period, Hegeman fought against the royalist Robles in Friesland, the rebel Schenk in Gelderland, and both Spanish and rebel troops (under Entens, see A1) in Holland. Most rebel ensigns of the early period were like this, with two or more bands in two to four colours.

F3: Captain Van den Tempel's ensign in 1580, from the De Gortter manuscript; this officer recaptured Mechelen from Spanish troops in that year. The diagonal stripe was inspired by Huguenot banners, and the crescent near the top of it refers to the crescent-shaped badges that 'beggars' started to wear in 1566 as a sign of rebel allegiance. The yellow letters '. L . T . D . P . ' stand for 'Liever Turks dan Paaps' ('Rather Turkish than Papist') – a fine example of the war of words often waged on banners of this period. Don Juan's banner at the battle of Gembloers in 1578 bore 'In hoc signo vici Turcos, in hoc vincam haereticos' ('In this sign I defeated the Turks, in this I will defeat the heretics').

F4: A Walloon company from Stead-Holder Rennenberg's force at the siege of Deventer, 1578, from a contemporary painting. The early army displayed many of these 'Burgundian cross' flags, since officially it still was loyal to the King of Spain. Rennenberg would soon show that loyalty by betraying the rebel cause and switching sides; he thus handed Spain the strategically important provinces of Groningen in the north-east and – through his family – Henegouwen (Hainaut) in the south-west.

F5: William Stewart's regiment in Mechelen, 1580, from the De Gortter manuscript. The source shows a yellowish orange, perhaps interpreting it as yet another orange-white-blue banner, but Stewart of Houston's livery colours were actually yellow, white and blue. (The banner of Capt Hoboken's company at the same date was illustrated with the same rounded fly, in 15 straight horizontal stripes – white, blue and orange repeated five times each.) Stewart's unit had fought in Zeeland, then went to Poland in 1577 to fight for King Stefan Batory at Danzig, before returning in 1579. It was merged with another Scottish unit in 1583, when Stewart returned to Scotland to become captain of the king's guard.

F6: Regulation ensign, North Holland Regiment, 1600 (reconstruction). In April 1591 it was decided that national and Scottish regiments should have ensigns bearing the red Dutch lion, and thereafter all new foreign regiments would carry these regulation flags. (This is the same lion that had become the country's coat of arms in September 1578, on a yellow field.) In March 1599 it was further decided that each regiment should have all its ensigns of the same basic colour, which implies that different companies within at least some regiments had previously used different colours. At first the lion had a crown and 17 arrows, one for each rebellious province; by 1591 it had lost ten of the arrows and its crown. The red lion's sword, arrows, claws and tongue would often be rendered in blue. Because it looked so much like the provincial coat of arms of Holland, it was decided in 1617 to reverse the colours: the United Provinces' banner would henceforth show a yellow lion on a red field, often with the details in white. New ensigns from that date on can be assumed to have borne the yellow lion. If a rectangular ensign was used, the lion was not usually placed centrally but closer to the hoist (pole).

F7: Company of Captain De Vries, 1605–16, from the sketches of Ernst Casimir of Nassau-Dietz (see under G).

F8: West Indies Company ensign, 1630s–40s, from a sketchbook in the New York Historical Society's collection. The GWC monogram is the abbreviation for Geoctrooieerde Westindische Compagnie ('Chartered West-Indies Company'). The sketchbook shows many company ensigns like this, using combinations of orange, blue, green and white, with four flames converging from the corners or the sides (some flames shorter than this example). Some have the coat of arms of one of the five WIC 'chambers' instead of the monogram.

F9: Civic Guard of Amsterdam, District 5, 1642, from a Backer painting. Civic guard ensigns show a wide variety, while those of paid militias were regulated and supplied by the government when the unit was created. For example, Holland's paid militia in 1596 had a 'traditional' orange-white-blue tricolour banner with the red national lion in the white band.

G: EVOLUTION: ERNST CASIMIR'S COMPANY ENSIGNS

Regulations clearly stated how an ensign of the standing army should look; however, many provincial units ignored these instructions despite several official requests. Among these were the units of Ernst Casimir, Count of Nassau-Dietz, who upon the death of William Louis succeeded him as Stead-Holder of Friesland, Groningen and Drenthe. In 1621, when hostilities resumed, he decided to create a unified design for the ensigns of the companies under his command. For units from his stead-holder provinces he chose blue and yellow, with the Frisian wreathed double lions (e.g. G2, G5 and G8), but for his own German units he used blue and white. His personal collection of sketches, with both the previously existing and the new designs, has been preserved, but never before published. This Men-at-Arms book is the first time any of those illustrated here have been seen in public, showing some unique examples of design evolution.

G1: Captain Atte Hettinga's company, *c.* 1615.
G2: Captain Atte Hettinga's company, 1620s.

Finely decorated powder flask, *c.* 1600; note the spring-loaded catch on the nozzle, enabling the musketeer to control the flow of powder. While flasks might be made of iron, wood or leather, materials which better resisted damp were superior, such as brass for the fittings, and for the body cow's horn, which could be softened in boiling water and then re-shaped as required. The large tasseled knots often illustrated at the ends of the suspension cord helped hold the flask steady. (RM)

G3: Captain Hennemarck's company from Ernst Casimir's own German regiment, 1620s.

G4: Captain Sageman's company, 1604–20. It is unclear from the sketch whether the ends of the individual stripes were cut in a dagged shape, merely represent wear-and-tear, or both. The crescent motif tells us that the captain used to be a 'sea-beggar'.

G5: Captain Sageman's company, after 1621.

G6: Captain Hanecrot's company, 1620s. He was the sergeant-major of Ernst Casimir's own German regiment.

G7: Captain Donia's company, 1610–21.

G8: Captain Donia's company, 1621–28, in which year another commander took over.

G9: Captain Resten's company, 1620s – another of Ernst Casimir's German companies.

H: BRAZIL, *c.* 1640
H1: European musketeer
H2: Mulatto musketeer

H3: Allied Tupi warrior
In the Americas, Africa and Asia Dutch activities were a mixture of trade and war, and from the start alliances were made with local rulers. In Brazil, European soldiers fought alongside mulatto musketeers and Indian warriors. The latter, mostly Tupis, proved decisive in at least one battle, and were an integral part of flying brigades and patrols hunting down Portuguese guerrillas. As part of the WIC's regular army they even accompanied the troops shipped to Angola. Elsewhere – in North America, Ghana, Sri Lanka, India, Taiwan and Indonesia – local allies helped the Dutch against local opponents only. In Asia the VOC organized civic guards in its new cities, composed of the same mix as the people living there; for example, the Batavia (Jakarta) civic guard had Dutch, Chinese and local members. Outside of Brazil, the only other non-European professional soldiery were the Japanese mercenaries working for the VOC; these proved just as troublesome as mercenaries back in Europe, being loyal only to whoever paid them the most and quickest.

INDEX

Figures in **bold** refer to images and captions.

12 Years' Truce, the 9, 10, 24, **33**
30 Years' War, the 7, 9, 10, 24
80 Years' War, the 2, 5, **6**, **7**, **8**, 9

Angola 10, **39**, 40, 47
Antwerp 3, 9, 10, **14**, 41
armour 15, **17**, 18, **23**, 24, 36, 40, 43, 44, 45
   half-armour **23**, 43, 45
army exercises 10, 16, 24
Arnhem **8**, 9, 10, 33

bandoleers 21, 23, 36, 44, 45
barber-surgeons 12, 18
beggars 4, **5**, 7, 9, 42, 46
   sea-beggars 3, 6, 9, 47
Bloody Council 5, 9
Brazil 10, **32**, 37, **39**, 40, 47
Breda 10, 34, 35, 42
brigades 20, 21, 24, **35**, **36**, 37
   flying brigades 34, 37, 45, 47
Brussels 4, **8**, 9
bucklers **17**, 23
   shotproof **17**, **23**;
      sword-and-buckler men 12, **17**, 18, 23, 44
bullets 15, **21**, 23, 36, 37, 40, 44

calivermen 11, 12, 13, 15, **17**, 18, 22, 23, **25**, **26**, 43, 44
calivers 7, 11, 15, 16, 18, 19, 20, 23
captains **6**, **7**, 11, 12, 14, 17, 18, 19, 33, 34, 36, 46, 47
   captain-generals 7, 19, **24**, 34
carabineers 34, 37, 45
Catholics 4, **5**, 6, 9
   Catholic League, the 10, 39
Civil War, 1568–87 9, 11, **25**, 38, 43, 46
Coalition War, 1621–48 10, 23, 24, **28**, **29**, 45
colonels 12, **17**, 18, **19**, 41, 45, 46
   lieutenant-colonels **17**, 19, 41
corporals 12, 15, **17**, 18, 22, 33
   lance-corporals 12, 13, **17**
corselets 15, 38, **44**

De Gheyn, Jacob **7**, 16, **38**
Den Briel 3, 5, 9, 43
deployment 20, 21, 22, **35**
disease **15**, 19, 24
dragoons **29**, 37, 44, 45
drill **4**, **7**, **16**, 17, 18, 19, 22, 24, 33, **34**, 35, **37**, **38**, 45
drummers **7**, 12, **14**, 16, **17**, 18, **19**, 23, 40

England 6, 7, 10, **24**, **34**, 38
ensigns **7**, 11, 12, 13, **17**, **19**, **27**, 33, 44, 45, 46
equipment 14, 15, 23, 24, 35, 38, 39, 45

fifers **7**, 12, 18, 23
firearms 11, 12, 13, 15, **18**, 20, 22, 23, 24, 33, **36**, 37, 40, 45
flags 11, **14**, **17**, **30**, **31**, 45, 46
flintlocks 33, 34, 36, 37, 40, 41, 44, 45
   companies 33, 35, 39, 40, 41
France 3, **4**, 6, 7, 9, 10, 11, 13, 19, 24, 34, 38, 39, 42
Friesland **11**, **16**, 17, 41, **45**, 46

Gembloers 9, **14**, 46
Germany **4**, **5**, **7**, 9, **11**, 12, 13, 19, 24, **36**, 39, 42, 43, 45, 46, 47
Ghent **8**, 9, **14**
Goes 9, 36, 43
gorget 23, 36, 38, 43, 44
Grave 10, **37**, 38
Groningen **8**, **11**, **16**, **17**, 41, 42, 43, **45**, 46
Guards Regiment, the 34, 37, 41, 45

Haarlem 6, 9, 43
Hague, The 7, **8**, 10, **12**, **23**, **24**, 33
halberdiers **12**, 13, 15, 18, 23, 41
halberds 11, **12**, **13**, 15, 18, 36, 43, 44
Heiligerlee **5**, 9, 13, 46
Henry, Frederick **4**, 7, 10, **12**, 21, **24**, **33**, 34, 36, 39, 41, 42, 45
heretics 5, 9, 46
Hertogenbosch **7**, 9, 10, 34, 42, 45
Hexham, Henry **4**, 34
Holland 3, **4**, 6, 9, 10, 11, 12, **13**, **14**, **15**, **16**, **17**, 19, 23, **33**, **34**, **36**, 37, 38, 39, 40, 41, 42, 43, 44, 45, 46, 47
Huguenots 9, 11, 38, 46
Hulst 10, **17**, 24

independence 4, 6, 9
   War for Independence, 1588–1620 10, 16, **26**, **27**, 44
Italy 4, **7**, 20, **43**

Leiden 2, 6, **8**, 9, 37, 38, 43, 44
lieutenants **6**, 12, **17**, 18, 33, **34**, 36
   lieutenant-colonels **17**, 19; lieutenant-generals 5, 12
Luanda **39**, 40

Maastricht **8**, 10, 41, 42
Madrid **2**, 4, 5, 7
manoeuvres 9, 10, 11, 16, **24**, 34
Mechelen 5, **8**, 9, 10, 43, 46
military **2**, **4**, **6**, 10, 11, **15**, **34**, 38, 40
militias (*waardgelders*) **37**, 38, 46
Mons 3, **8**, 45
Mookerheide 9, 14, **37**
Mulatto **32**, 40, 47
musketeers 12, 13, 15, **17**, 18, **19**, 21, 23, **27**, **28**, **29**, 34, 35, 36, 39, 40, 44, 45, **47**
muskets 7, 11, 15, 16, **18**, **19**, **20**, 21, 23, 24, 33, 36, 44, 45
   Matchlock 15, **18**, **35**, 37, 40
mutiny 11, 13, 24

Naarden 5, **8**, 9
Nassau-Dietz, Ernst Casimir, Count of **45**, 46
Nassau-Dillenburg, William Louis, Count of **16**, 17, 22, **38**, 41, 42, 43, 46
Nassau-Siegen, John VII, Count of 19, 20, 21, 34, 36, **38**, 45
Netherlands, the 3, **4**, **5**, 6, 7, 9, 10, **24**, 36, 45
Nieuwpoort **2**, 10, 18, 21, 44

officers **4**, **6**, 11, 12, 15, 16, **17**, **18**, 21, 23, 24, **25**, **28**, 33, 34, 38, 39, 43, 45, 46
Orange, William of **2**, **4**, **5**, **7**, 9, 10, 11, **12**, 41
organization 11, 12, 14, 16, 18, 33, 45

partisans 15, 36, 43, 45
Philip II, King of Spain 4, **5**, 6, 9, 10, 46

pikemen 12, 13, 15, **17**, 18, 19, 20, 21, 22, 23, 24, **26**, **27**, **28**, **33**, 36, 40, **44**, 45
pikes **7**, 12, **14**, 15, **17**, 18, **19**, 20, **23**, 33, **36**, 45
   pike and shot **14**, 18, **39**; pike blocks 13, **17**, **19**, 20, 21, 24, **35**, 45
plates **7**, **14**, 15, 23, 37, **38**, **43**, 45
   breast-and-back **17**, 23, 36, 43, 44, 45
plumes **6**, 15, 23, 43, 44
plundering 3, **7**, 11, 24, 37
politics **2**, **5**, 6, 7, 19
Portugal **39**, 40, 47
Prince of Orange, Count of Nassau, Maurice **2**, **4**, **6**, **7**, 10, 11, **12**, **16**, **17**, 18, **19**, 20, 21, 22, **23**, **24**, **33**, 34, 35, 36, 37, **38**, 39, 41, 42, 44, 45
Protestants **4**, **5**, 6, 9, 10, 11, **38**, 39, 43
provosts 12, 18, 19

quartermasters **2**, 12, 18, 19

Republic of the Seven United Netherlands (the United Provinces), the 7, 9, 10, 22, **24**, 38, 39, 41, 46
Robles, Caspar de **11**, 46

sashes 15, 23, 35, 42, 44, 45
sergeants **7**, 11, 12, **13**, 15, **17**, 18, **26**, 33, **34**, 36, 44
   sergeant-majors **7**, 12, **17**, 19, 41, 47
servants (*knechts*) 12, 18
skirmishers (*vuurroer*) 10, **29**, 33, 35, 37, 40, 41, 45
snaphaunce **18**, 23, 36, 37, 45
soldiers **5**, 6, **7**, 9, 12, 14, **15**, 16, 18, 19, **23**, 35, 37, 38, 40, 47
Spain **2**, 3, 4, **5**, 6, **7**, 9, 10, 11, 13, **15**, 21, 24, 33, 34, **36**, 38, 39, 40, **43**, 46
States' Army (*Staatse Leger*), the **6**, 7, **34**, 38, 45
States General, the 4, 7, 9, 10, 12, 41
Stead-Holder (*Stadhouder*) 7, 10, **11**, **16**, **24**, 41, 43, **45**, 46
Stevin, Simon **2**, 21
sutlers **15**, 18
Sweden 10, 24, **29**, **36**, **38**, 45
swordsmen 12, 15, **23**, 24

targeteers 12, **17**
tassets 23, 36, 38, 44, 45
Toledo, Don Fernando Alvarez de, Duke of Alva 3, 4, **5**, 6, **7**, 9, 46
training 16, 39
Triple Alliance 7, 10
Tupis **32**, 47

United East Indies Company (VOC), the 10, **39**, 40, 47
Utrecht 3, 8, 9, 10, 41

Venice 39, 46
Vere, Francis **17**, 19, 20, 42

Walloons **11**, 13, 42, 46
West Indies Company (WIC), the 10, **39**, 40, 46
wheellocks 15, **18**, 23, 37, 44

Zeeland 3, 12, **14**, 36, 41, 46